"The problem of stress and anxiety is everywhere today—in all corners and age groups. To resist anxiety's power, Will Dickerson shows us the need to understand and live out a biblical shalom. Shalom shows us a way of seeing the world and its meaning as a foundation from which to face the difficult and unexpected with purpose and hope. He does this by giving us fresh ways to understand biblical texts while also connecting them to the depth of the larger Christian story."

—DICK KEYES
Former Director, L'Abri Fellowship, Massachusetts

"Will Dickerson has provided a keen and much needed insight into the 'full and meaningful life' which comes to us through the Hebrew and Christian faiths. His own personal journey is inspired and inspiring. His thirty years as a Christian teacher to students reared under atheistic Communism provides him a keen insight lacking to most 'westerners.' His theological depth on subjects like 'heaven and hell' give us a much-needed textbook. His clarity of writing makes his book appealing to a diverse audience."

—DONALD W. HAYNES
Retired Professor of Wesleyan Theology, Hood Theological Seminary

"In our often jangled and frenzied quest for peace and rest, Will Dickerson is a humble shepherd shining the light of scripture and the lessons of history into the dark places where the monsters that frighten us reside. With the skill of a seasoned teacher, he guides us with honesty and hope. *The Search for Shalom* is not a fix-it manual. Instead imagine stepping into a gallery, a museum of grace in which our author points at times to a story, there to a poem, and here to a song. Gradually as our racing heart subsides and our eyes adjust to the softer light, we begin to discover that we are inhabiting that place for which our souls long so deeply and desperately. We find ourselves in the Savior's embrace. Shalom."

—STEVE FROEHLICH
Grace Unscripted website

"Simple truths, profound challenge. This book explores many simple and clear teachings of the Bible such as patience, forgiveness, generosity, reconciliation—and why living them is harder than understanding them. With honesty and hope, it invites readers to consider how love for God shapes not just what we believe, but who we become. A call to authentic faith formed by character, not convenience."

—JEFFRY MAX EDWARDS
President, One Mission Society

The Search for Shalom

The Search for Shalom

The Quest for Peace in an Age of High Anxiety

WILL DICKERSON

WIPF & STOCK · Eugene, Oregon

THE SEARCH FOR SHALOM
The Quest for Peace in an Age of High Anxiety

Wipf & Stock
An Imprint of Wipf and Stock Publishers
199 W. 8th Ave., Suite 3
Eugene, OR 97401

www.wipfandstock.com

PAPERBACK ISBN: 979-8-3852-4938-1
HARDCOVER ISBN: 979-8-3852-4939-8
EBOOK ISBN: 979-8-3852-4940-4

VERSION NUMBER 053025

The song lyrics to "No Other Name" by Matthew Dickerson ©2015 are
used by permission. All rights reserved.

Scripture quotations taken from the (NASB®) New American Standard
Bible®, Copyright © 2020 by The Lockman Foundation. Used by permission. All rights reserved. www.lockman.org

All websites listed herein are accurate at the time of publication but may
change in the future or cease to exist. The listing of website references and
resources does not imply publisher endorsement of the site's entire con-
tents. Groups and organizations are listed for informational purposes, and
listing does not imply publisher endorsement of their activities.

soli Deo gloria

Contents

Man is one of your creatures, Lord, and it is his nature to praise You. He bears upon himself the mark of death, the sign of his own sin, to remind him that You stand against the proud. Nevertheless, since he is part of Your creation, his desire is to praise You. The thought of You stirs him so deeply that he can not be at peace unless he praises You. For You made us for Yourself, and our hearts will not find peace until they rest in You.

AUGUSTINE, *CONFESSIONS* 1.1

Preface

MANY AN ANALYST HAS noted that we live in an age of high anxiety. As a testament to this fact, we can walk into almost any bookstore and find shelves of books documenting our anxious condition, providing in-depth analyses, and offering a variety of self-help cures. The book you are now reading is not a self-help book. In fact, it will make the argument that self-guided efforts to treat this ailment of the soul will only serve to make the condition worse. The search for shalom—a deep, all-encompassing peace—must lead us elsewhere.

Yogi Berra once said, "You got to be very careful if you don't know where you're going because you might not get there."[1] On another occasion he remarked, "We may be lost but we're making good time."[2] Both quips have more than a touch of humor in them. Unfortunately, both sayings also serve as fitting descriptions of modern society. We are lost, and yet we are speeding along at a frenetic pace in our terrible hurry to get somewhere. Meanwhile, since we don't have the slightest idea of where we are going, we are not getting any closer to anywhere we want to be.

People say they want to be happy. To be happy, they say they need to be at peace. They are not talking about living under a temporary ceasefire, or the temporary cessation of hostilities, but about a deep inner peace. They want what is known in Hebrew as "shalom." Jesus came to bring this peace. He came to reconcile

1. Barra, *Yogi Berra*, 398.
2. Barra, *Yogi Berra*, 397.

God and man so that we can once again know God's extravagant love.

Many people, however, have been scammed by Satan, the prince of scammers. As a result, they don't give much attention to the one who can actually bring them true peace. Instead, they continue to be controlled by their fears and anxieties. They spend their lives in the service of various idols, the most popular of which is Mammon. They nurture their grudges, refuse to forgive, and they live in the rubble of broken relationships. Some people give lip service to the fact that God is on the throne, but instead of serving as ministers of reconciliation, they enlist as soldiers in the culture wars and end up spending their lives fighting the wrong battles with the wrong weapons. As a result, most of us live in a state of war. We are at war on multiple levels, from the intrapersonal to the international, and we have no peace. We are driven by our fears and anxieties. We should not be surprised, therefore, when we read that the use of antidepressants and antianxiety medications has exploded in recent decades.

So where can we find peace? Who has the road map?

Acknowledgments

SEVERAL PEOPLE MADE IMPORTANT contributes to the writing of this book. I owe a debt of gratitude to each of them.

I am thankful to Tawny Johnson for reading and editing an early version of this book. She made several very good suggestions that led to the improvement of this work. I am also thankful to Bill Murphy and Wayne Parker who took the time to read the manuscript at a somewhat later stage and to offer their feedback.

I very much appreciate the time given and the effort made by Rev. Don Haynes and my sister-in-law Deborah Dickerson to proofread the text. Not only did they find numerous typographical errors, but they made several suggestions of substance that made the work much better. I think the message is a bit clearer now because of them

Most of all, I am grateful to my wonderful wife, Julia. She gave me helpful input at an early stage of my writing and then put up with me during the last few years while the book was slowly taking shape.

Despite the best efforts of my friends and family, the reader will likely find errors both great and small in this book. That is completely my fault.

Introduction

Spiritual Geography

NOWADAYS, MANY OF US live lives marked by a notable absence of peace. The news never fails to remind us that nations are at war with other nations. Many of us, in one way or another, are at war with the people around us. And increasingly, we find that we are at war within ourselves. As a result, we have no peace. Rather, we live in a state of war.

In order to understand this state in which we find ourselves, we must survey the spiritual landscape; for the conflict in which we are immersed is not just of a physical nature. As the apostle Paul tells us, we do not wrestle primarily against flesh and blood, but against a spiritual enemy (Eph 6:12). If we can recognize that we are at war and that this war is of a spiritual nature, we can learn much from those great military leaders who, prior to meeting the enemy on the field of battle, would make every effort to familiarize themselves with the terrain on which their contests would be decided. Whenever possible, these leaders would choose the ground on which the battle would be waged and would prepare it ahead of time in order to make the enemy fight on their terms and to give their own forces the greatest possible advantage. Let us, therefore, take a look at a spiritual map. Let us look at heaven, hell, and earth, and at their relative positions to one another so that we might better know the terrain on which we fight our battles.

I do not hold what I am about to say as a doctrine of first importance or as one that a person must accept in order to be saved. Therefore, I won't be offended if folks disagree with me over what follows. Nevertheless, I am persuaded that this survey is well-grounded in Scripture and in the historical beliefs of the church.

Spiritual Geography

Many people envision a scenario in which heaven is located somewhere above, earth is in the middle, and hell is somewhere down below. Heaven is where God and the angels reside; hell is where Satan and the demons make their abode; and earth is neutral territory in between, which we humans and all other flesh inhabit. According to this scheme, both the demons and angels have to grab their lunch pails and commute to work each day in their efforts to lead us either to perdition or salvation. When we die, our souls then rise to heaven or sink to hell depending on whether we are right with God. Those who descend to hell suffer unspeakable torture and pain, while those who ascend to heaven get wings and harps and join the celestial choir. This scenario, however, is not really biblical. Rather, it is based on old pagan beliefs that came to us by way of the Anglo-Saxons and other northern European tribes.

Sheol

In Old Testament times, the Israelites believed that when the body died the soul went to a place called Sheol. This is a place where our spirits, or shadows, rest until the day of judgment. Unlike the pagan concept of hell, Sheol is not a place of torment. Rather it is a place of rest or sleep. Moreover, we are told that God is present, even in Sheol. For example, Ps 139:8 declares, "If I ascend to heaven, You are there; if I make my bed in Sheol, behold, You are there." Likewise, Ps 86:13 (which is a Messianic prophecy) says, "Your graciousness toward me is great, and You have saved my soul from the depths of Sheol." Sheol is also implied in Ps 23:4 (another Messianic prophecy), in which the speaker declares that God is with him even if he walks through "the valley of the shadow of death," a poetic reference to Sheol.

The early church taught that Jesus himself spent time in Sheol between his crucifixion and resurrection. Indeed, Ps 86:13 tells us that God the Father will rescue the Messiah from Sheol. In Greek, Sheol was translated as Hades. Sometimes, it was also personified as Death. In the first century AD, it was commonly believed that this place where the dead rested was divided into two subdivisions: paradise was the nicer neighborhood where the righteous rested, while the wicked were sent across the tracks to a much less comfortable area sometimes called Abaddon, or "the pit." Paradise was not the same place as heaven. Rather, it was where the souls of the righteous rested until the day of judgment. When Jesus was crucified, he told the thief on the cross next to him that they would see each other in paradise later that very day. According to 1 Pet 3:18–20, upon his crucifixion Jesus preached to the souls in Sheol who were being held captive there by death. The Apostles Creed, which was originally written in Greek, affirms that Jesus descended into Hades (that is, Sheol) after he was crucified.[1] He was then raised from the dead on the third day.

The early Christians believed that when the body died, the soul rested, or slept, in Hades (Sheol) until the day of judgment, at which time the trumpet shall sound and the dead shall be raised. In fact, the English term "cemetery" comes from the Greek word *koimeterion* (κοιμητηριον), which literally means a "sleeping place."[2] This is the reason why you can find the words "rest in peace" in cemeteries around the world wherever Christians are buried.

Gehenna

The Bible does speak of a place of pain and torment. This is Gehenna. Gehenna is cited in both the Old and New Testaments, as well as in early Christian writing, as the final destination of the wicked. On the day of judgment, this is where they will be sent

---

1. Logos Staff, "Apostles' Creed," para. 9.
2. Wiktionary, "κοιμητήριον."

for punishment or destruction. Gehenna is not the same place as Sheol.

Hell

In the Middle Ages, prior to their encounter with Christianity, the pagan tribes of northern Europe commonly believed that those who did not do good here on earth would be sent to a place of torment immediately upon their death. As you might imagine, these pagans did not always define good the same way we do. Nevertheless, they believed that those who did not do good would be punished. In the Anglo-Saxon language (otherwise known as Old English) this place of punishment was called hell. As Christianity gained a foothold in Europe and made converts, especially among the tribes of northern Europe, often a degree of syncretism occurred. The Anglo-Saxon cosmology did not have separate concepts or words that corresponded with Sheol and Gehenna. As a result, both Sheol (Hades) and Gehenna were translated into Old English as "hell." When this was done, the Anglo-Saxon ideas about hell more or less remained attached to the vocabulary and replaced the Hebrew notions. As the classical scholar James J. O'Donnell observes,

> Whatever core ideas Christianity sought to transmit, every baptism brought someone unshaped by Christianity into the fold, mixing their ideas and expectations with what they found. The pristine essence of Christianity acquired a lot of old-fashioned baggage along the way.[3]

Over time, Sheol and Gehenna, which were two very distinct places in the Judeo-Christian cosmology, were conflated into the single Anglo-Saxon concept of hell as more and more northern Europeans converted to Christianity.

A second reason why Sheol and Gehenna were merged into a single place of torment was the development of the Catholic doctrine of Purgatory in the twelfth century. As the Catholic Church

---

3. O'Donnell, *Pagans*, 4.

developed its sacramental theology during the course of the Middle Ages, it found it needed a place to put those who remained securely within the fold of the Catholic Church, but who had not yet made atonement for their venial sins. Therefore, the idea of a temporary transfer station between heaven and hell was revived. However, Sheol, which was a place of rest, was transformed into a place where the souls of believers are required to do penance for their venial sins before they can gain admission to heaven.

Earth

So, if the Bible does not teach us that Satan and the demons reside in hell, just where do they live? In fact, Scripture indicates that earth is their home. Ever since the fall, this corner of creation has been under their dominion! In Luke 4:6, for example, Satan boasts that this world, and all that is in it, is his, and he tells Jesus that he will hand it over to him if Jesus will simply bow down and worship him. 1 John 5:19 confirms "that the whole world lies in the power of the evil one." And in Eph 2:2, Paul tells us that Satan is the "prince of the power of the air." Other texts in Scripture also speak of Satan's dominion over this world (see, for example, John 12:31; 14:30; 16:11; and 2 Cor 4:4). The first two chapters of Genesis tell us how he came into possession of the earth.

Seen from this perspective, perhaps we could view the incarnation of Christ as the equivalent of a spiritual D-Day. God established a beachhead on occupied territory (Satan's domain on earth) and began the process of liberating the earth. Some years later, when Jesus sent his disciples out to preach the kingdom of heaven, he said, "I watched Satan fall from heaven like lightning" (Luke 10:18). When he sent his disciples out to spread the gospel, Jesus started the process of dislodging Satan from the territory he had occupied at the time of the fall.

We should be careful, however, when we use this sort of military analogy; for the Lord did not intend for us to fight the good fight with the weapons typically used in secular struggles for power. We should not allow ourselves to get caught up in the rhetoric of the culture wars; for Jesus consistently maintained that his kingdom was not of this world, and he refused to take up arms or make use of political power to achieve his ends. His weapons were the cross and selfless love. Indeed, he tells us that we must love—even our enemies.[4]

Some Practical Implications

So, what does all this mean for us in practical terms? For one thing, it means that we are not living on neutral ground. All of us, regardless of where on earth we live, are behind the front lines and in enemy territory. We are living in a fallen world. Therefore, we should not suffer the illusion that we are living in a Christian nation that needs to be defended from the ungodly. Nor should we be shocked when we see evidence of the devil's handiwork all around us. In fact, this is what should be expected. Nevertheless, we ought not tremble in fear or cower behind defensive barricades. We may live in a world that is enshrouded in spiritual darkness, but we have been given a mandate to be light! We have been called to help others see.

A few summers ago, my wife and I were able to spend some days with my brother and his wife in Portland, Maine. While we were there, they took us to see the Portland Head Lighthouse. The lighthouse was originally commissioned by George Washington back in 1790, and it has been providing light to sailors ever since. There is a bronze plaque on the wall of the lighthouse that lists the names of the first two dozen or so lighthouse keepers. It refers to these people as "Keepers of the Light." I like that title. And it seems to me that all of us who are followers of Christ should in some sense be keepers of the light. We should all be shining our light and doing our best to prevent others from running aground in the dark.

4. C. S. Lewis explores God's use of love as his primary weapon in an amusing way in chapter 19 of *The Screwtape Letters*. See also Dickerson, *Fingerprint of God*.

Unfortunately, the spirit of darkness, with its air of hopelessness and despair, is often overwhelming to those imprisoned by it. This seems to be particularly true in Hungary where I lived and taught for over thirty years. There, pessimism is a powerful force, and suicide rates historically have ranked among the highest in the world. However, even in the US—the land of milk and honey—despair is on the rise. So, how can we serve as keepers of the light in this dark world in which we reside?

Portland Head Light, Portland, Maine

The Hold-fast

by

George Herbert (1633)

I threaten'd to observe the strict decree
    Of my dear God with all my power and might;
    But I was told by one it could not be;
Yet I might trust in God to be my light.
"Then will I trust," said I, "in Him alone."
    "Nay, e'en to trust in Him was also His:
    We must confess that nothing is our own."
"Then I confess that He my succour is."
"But to have nought is ours, not to confess
    That we have nought." I stood amaz'd at this,
    Much troubled, till I heard a friend express
That all things were more ours by being His;
    What Adam had, and forfeited for all,
    Christ keepeth now, who cannot fail or fall.

1

War

For the creation was subjected to futility, not willingly, but because of Him who subjected it, in hope that the creation itself also will be set free from its slavery to corruption into the freedom of the glory of the children of God. For we know that the whole creation groans and suffers the pains of childbirth together until now.

ROMANS 8:20–22

MY WIFE GREW UP in Asheboro, North Carolina. Her mom still makes her home there. In fact, she still lives in the same house that my wife grew up in. The house was built in a quiet neighborhood on the outskirts of town, and it is situated on a wooded lot that overlooks a small pond. One of the nicest features of the home is a spacious screened porch that faces the woods and looks down over the pond's normally tranquil waters. The place is teeming with wildlife: deer, squirrels, rabbits, turtles, toads, salamanders, bugs of all shapes and sizes, and birds—lots of birds.

The porch is a wonderful place to read the Bible, pray, and meditate, especially if I can get out there before everyone else wakes up and gets going. But even if others are already up, the porch is always quiet, and it is a great place to do my daily devotional reading. In fact, the only thing that sometimes keeps me from hearing myself think is all the ruckus the birds are making. My mother-in-law keeps a couple of well-stocked bird feeders in the backyard, so every morning one can see a crowd of feathered commuters hovering about trying to grab a quick breakfast before they fly off to do whatever birds do during the day. There is also an abundance of squirrels. These squirrels are constantly looking for an opportunity to dash in and pilfer some choice seeds.

I am no ornithologist, but I am pretty sure I have seen chickadees, nuthatches, tufted titmice, bluebirds, cardinals, at least two types of woodpeckers, at least three types of hummingbirds, and even a yellow-bellied sapsucker dining on the fine offerings dispensed by those bird feeders. I have also seen several other species of birds at the feeders whose genus I do not know. Last summer, a murder of crows took up residence somewhere in the neighborhood, and they could often be heard conversing among themselves. Moreover, while sitting on the porch, I have seen larger birds of prey (big hawks of some sort and an owl) hunting for food in the woods down by the pond. When my wife and I go for evening walks around the neighborhood, we frequently see flocks of swallows on duty in the sky above us. From the looks of things, they are doing their best to protect us from the onslaught of North Carolina's bug population. The swallows normally stay on the job until dusk. That is when they punch out and the bats report for duty. I know that technically bats are not birds (they are flying mammals); nevertheless, they have managed to carve out a useful niche for themselves there among the local avian population.

I have often heard people wistfully say they would love to be "as free and as carefree as a bird." However, after watching these feathered members of the animal kingdom dine over the course of several summers, I have observed that they never really are at rest. They are always on the lookout for some creature higher up the food chain that might want to make a meal out of them. The birds at the bird feeder, for example, constantly flit about, nervously looking all around them with rapid, agitated movements. Frequently, as they are getting ready to snatch a bite from one of the feeders, they are spooked by some imaginary threat lurking nearby and quickly dart back to the cover of the woods before they have a chance to grab a choice seed or two. Similarly, the slightest noise or movement causes squirrels and rabbits to freeze in their tracks. The little critters stand motionless for a time, cautiously scanning the perimeter for predators, all the while formulating plans for a rapid escape in the event one is detected. If I make even the slightest movement, the animals sprint for cover. Even the big birds of prey, the hawks and the owls, are often frightened by movements in the forest and suddenly flee to a place of greater safety.

People, therefore, may imagine that it would be wonderful to be "as free as a bird" and be able to soar about wherever and whenever they want; however, I would question whether birds really are that free. Indeed, upon closer examination, our feathered friends, as well as the other members of the wildlife population, all appear to be prisoners of some kind. They seem to be prisoners of fear—for they live in a dog-eat-dog world in which they can never let their guard down. They never know when some predator further up the food chain will appear and attempt to make a meal out of them. As a result, they must be ever vigilant, and they never experience true peace. They live their entire lives in a constant state of war—one in which might makes right.

Last summer, my wife and I spent several weeks at my brother's home in Vermont. While we were there, I noticed that two robins had built a nest in the apple tree just outside our bedroom

window. Later, when the parents were making a grocery run—
presumably checking out the selection of worms, grubs, and bugs
in the nearby garden—I discovered that the couple was attempting to raise not just one, but three newly hatched chicks. These
youngsters were quite hungry and couldn't wait for their parents
to return with some fresh treats.

I was captivated by this miracle of birth, growth, and life. On
several occasions, I just sat and watched the nest for a period of
time. It was beautiful to behold. But one day, while I was looking
up at the nest from the ground below, I saw the black silhouettes of
seven large turkey vultures flying overhead. They reminded me of
the Ring Wraiths in Tolkien's *Lord of the Rings*. They appeared to
be scanning the landscape for some putrid, decomposing carrion
on which they could feast. I was suddenly reminded that death is
very much a part of this broken world in which we live. Indeed, it
holds great power over us.

I do not know the metaphysical laws that subjected all of creation to the power of death. C. S. Lewis, in his *Chronicles of Nar-
nia*, would have referred to these laws as "the deeper magic."[1] I do
know, however, that Scripture indicates this world is now in Satan's
hands. As already mentioned, in Eph 2:2 Paul refers to our spiritual enemy as "the prince of the power of the air." In John 12:31
Jesus himself calls Satan "the ruler of this world." And when Satan
tempted Jesus in the desert, Satan boasted that all the kingdoms of
the world had been given to him and that he could give them to
whomever he pleased (Luke 4:5–6).

It is clear, not only from Scripture, but also from the evidence
we see all around us, that we live in a very broken world, a world
in which death reigns. The apostle Paul, in Rom 8:19–22, made
reference to this fact when he wrote,

> For the eagerly awaiting creation waits for the revealing
> of the sons and daughters of God. For the creation was
> subjected to futility, not willingly, but because of Him
> who subjected it, in hope that the creation itself also will
> be set free from its slavery to corruption into the freedom

1. Lewis, *Lion*, ch. 13, 15.

of the glory of the children of God. For we know that the
whole creation groans and suffers the pains of childbirth
together until now.

All of creation, even the birds and squirrels, groans and suffers as
it waits for God to end the state of war in which it finds itself and
to restore creation to what it was meant to be.

Like the members of the animal kingdom mentioned above,
most humans also live in fear of one kind or another. Very few of
us are truly at peace. In fact, those who study human psychology
have observed that much of what humans do and say is driven
by fear. Politicians certainly know this, for most political campaigns are carefully crafted to stoke the flames of fear. Political ads
speak in apocalyptic terms when they tell you that this is the most
important campaign in history and that the candidate from the
opposition party will do great evil if elected. Indeed, civilization
as we know it will assuredly end in a terrible conflagration if the
opposition should ever come to power. Be afraid—be very afraid,
and vote for our candidate if you want to save the world.

Even those who consider themselves to be followers of Christ
often live in the grip of this fear. They read Revelation and other
passages in Scripture that foretell a time of great persecution, and
they tremble. They forget that these books were written to assure
us that God will see us through these difficult times. These proph-
ecies were meant to strengthen our faith in God. Instead, many
let their fears control them, and rather than putting their trust in
Christ, they put it in the secular rulers of this age—kings, presi-
dents, and every variety of political scoundrel who would prey on
their fears. As a result, these Christians at times forge some very
unholy alliances.

In the Old Testament, time and again the Israelites put their
trust in kings and men at arms, despite the warnings they received
from prophets not to do so. This strategy did not work out very
well for them. It will not turn out well for us either. These secular
rulers and politicians cannot save us, and they cannot prevent the
word of God from being realized.

Governments around the world spend billions—perhaps trillions—of dollars in efforts to bolster their law enforcement agencies and their militaries. At any given moment, dozens of armed conflicts are raging in various parts of the globe.

On a more personal level, many people live in fear of physical harm. Even if we do not live in a war zone, we are afraid that someone might rob us or do us great injury. Not surprisingly, the sale of security services, not to mention of firearms, has become a multibillion-dollar industry. These days, many people also fear that they will fall victim to one form of pestilence or another. Hence, insurance companies are earning record profits as people seek protection from the ravages of disease. Some people are controlled by other kinds of phobias. They are afraid of heights, or of spiders, or of being in small spaces, and so forth. And it is not uncommon for people to be afraid that they won't have enough money in the future, or that they will lose their job and not be able to pay their bills.

As a society, we struggle mightily with the fear of those who do not look, or think, or behave the same way we do. We speak about the virtues of love and toleration, but often we only bestow these blessings on those who look like us and who hold the same beliefs we do. Others we look at askance. Quite possibly, we see ourselves as combatants in what has been called the culture wars, and so we dig in behind an array of defensive barriers and prepare for what we believe is the inevitable assault by the unfaithful and unorthodox.

Sometimes our fears lie within the deeper recesses of the soul. We are afraid of rejection, of embarrassment, or of injury to our pride. We are afraid that we will lose face. Many are afraid of failure, or that their lives might turn out to be meaningless. Hence, psychologists have observed that we have developed a multitude of defense mechanisms to prevent us from being hurt and to prevent our fears from being realized. We put up protective walls around us to insulate us from the things we fear—often at the expense of cutting ourselves off from the people around us.

Like the birds and other wildlife in my in-laws' backyard, we are constantly flitting about, nervously looking all around us with rapid, agitated movements. Our defenses are up as we seek to protect ourselves from whatever predators are further up the food chain—whether at the personal, societal, or global level. We groan together with all of creation as we look for respite from this war in which we find ourselves mired. But this is not the way God intended us to live our lives!

Be Thou My Vision

Traditional Irish hymn
Translated by Mary Elizabeth Byrne
Versified by Eleanor Hull

Be Thou my vision, O Lord of my heart;
Naught be all else to me save that Thou art.
Thou my best thought by day and by night;
Waking or sleeping, thy presence my light.

Be Thou my wisdom, and thou my true Word;
I ever with thee and thou with me, Lord.
Thou my great Father, I thy dear child;
Thou in me dwelling, with thee reconciled.

Be thou my breastplate, my sword for the fight;
Be thou my dignity, thou my delight.
Thou my soul's shelter, thou my high tow'r,
Raise thou me Heav'nward, O Pow'r of my pow'r.

Riches I heed not, nor vain, empty praise;
Thou mine inheritance, now and always.
Thou and thou only, first in my heart,
High King of Heaven, my treasure thou art.

High King of Heaven, my victory won,
May I reach Heaven's joys, O bright Heav'ns Sun!
Heart of my heart, whatever befall,
Still be my vision, O Ruler of all.

2

The Enemy

For our struggle is not against flesh and blood, but against the rulers, against the powers, against the world forces of this darkness, against the spiritual forces of wickedness in the heavenly places.

EPHESIANS 6:12

PAUL TELLS US THAT we are engaged in a mighty struggle. However, he informs us that our enemy is not an earthly foe. Our struggle is not against "flesh and blood." Rather, we are engaged in a battle against spiritual forces.

In any conflict, it is important to know who the enemy is. It is just as important to know who our enemy is not. Indeed, there is something particularly tragic about casualties that are killed or wounded by friendly fire. We need to remind ourselves, therefore, that our enemy is not the aggressive driver who cut us off during rush hour. It is not the person who is rude to us at the supermarket. It is not the person whose political, ideological, or theological views differ from ours. It is not even the person who may do us actual harm. As followers of Christ, we must keep this in mind and not treat such people as though they were the real enemies. Moreover, Jesus tells us that even if they were the real enemies, we must still love them. These are all people we must love.

As Paul writes, our fight is against "the rulers, against the powers, against the world forces of this darkness, against the spiritual forces of wickedness in the heavenly places." The chief of these spiritual forces of wickedness is Satan. The Bible does not really tell us all that much about our enemy. One reason for this is that we ought not give Satan the attention he so desperately longs for. He is, after all, the father of all narcissists. A second, and more important, reason is that we need to keep our eyes focused on Christ. If our gaze remains on Jesus, he will lead us safely through this present conflict, and we will not be unsettled by any of our enemy's tactics. We should not be giving the enemy undue attention, nor should we be trembling at his power.

It is true that the enemy is the temporary master of this world. As such, he has a wide variety of resources at his disposal; and although he does use a multiplicity of means to accomplish his goals, he relies primarily on two main stratagems: deceit and accusation.

In John 8:44, Jesus calls Satan "the father of lies." We can read his first lie in Gen 3:2–4. Eve explains to the serpent, "From the fruit of the trees of the garden we may eat; but from the fruit of the tree which is in the middle of the garden, God has said, 'You shall not eat from it or touch it, or you will die.'" The serpent then responds with the original lie, "You certainly will not die!" Eve believed this lie, and soon thereafter death entered our world.

Today, Satan continues to use this same strategy of deceitful denial with great effect. The Bible tells us many things very clearly and in plain and direct language. However, Satan whispers in our ears, "That is not true! That statement you read in the Bible is really just a long-outdated vestige of ancient culture. We can disregard it and concentrate on the real message of Scripture. As enlightened intellectuals of the twenty-first century, we know better than to take such cultural baggage at face value. God didn't really mean that . . ." So, peace continues to elude us.

Of course, the denial of Biblical truth is not the only lie that Satan spews. He has a whole arsenal of lies, many of which are personally tailored for the specific individual. He knows our weaknesses and where we are fragile, and he will try to attack us at our most vulnerable point. For example, if you struggle with acceptance, he will tell you, "God couldn't possibly love you! You are not good enough. You are hopelessly tainted by the wreckage of your inglorious past. You must work harder and do more in order to earn God's approval." Maybe you have heard such lies? Maybe you have even believed them?

If, on the other hand, your struggle is with pride, then Satan will likely come at you from the opposite direction. He might whisper into your heart, "You are better than that multitude of losers. It is true you may have made a few small mistakes here and there, but compared to the unwashed rabble, you are a saint. Compared to the ignorant, you are a paragon of knowledge. You are truly deserving of your place in the celestial choir. You have little need of God's grace. Rather, you need to be given the credit you deserve." Have you ever heard this lie whispered in the inner recesses of your heart?

What are some of the other lies that Satan employs to trip us up? For one, Satan lies to us about God. He tells us that God is like an angry judge who is just waiting for us to slip up so that he can unleash his wrath upon us. He tells us that God is restricting our freedom and preventing us from enjoying life. He tells us that God does not really love us.

When we hear these lies whispered in the dark recesses of our souls, we must remember the truth. The truth is that Jesus allowed himself to be nailed to a cross because he loves you with a love that is too deep to fathom. Keep in mind that when Satan tempted Jesus in the desert, he mentioned how the angels would obey every command that Jesus gave them. They would keep him from stumbling, and they would bear him up and prevent him from suffering harm on the rocks if he were to fall. We know, therefore, that when Jesus was led to Calvary, had he chosen to, with a single word he could have ordered a legion of angels to deliver him from his executioners. He very easily could have avoided that most excruciating episode on the cross. But he never uttered that word, even as the Roman soldiers were driving nails through his hands and feet! Why did Jesus remain silent?

Physically speaking, it is true that the nails fixed his body to the cross. We can use the laws of physics to calculate the forces of friction that kept the nails from slipping out of the wood and that allowed those same nails to hold his bones and flesh in place. However, it was actually his love for you that kept him there on the cross! He could have commanded the angels to rescue him, but he didn't. The reason he didn't is because Jesus loves you with a mad, passionate love—a love beyond the power of our human words to describe—and he wants to spend all eternity with you. That is the reason he remained on the cross until he breathed his last and gave up his spirit. He loves you! Never let Satan's lies cause you to doubt God's boundless love for you.

Satan is also known as "The Accuser." In fact, his name means "accuser."[1] In Greek, he is often referred to as "diablos," from which we get the English "devil." Diablos means "slanderer."[2] One of Satan's primary tactics, in addition to his spinning of lies, is to hurl accusations against us and to slander us.

1. Kelly, *Satan*, 16.

2. Etymonline, "Devil (n.)," paras. 1–2.

If you are familiar with the story of Job, you know that Job was a righteous man. He was also very prosperous. So, Satan went before God time and again to slander Job and bring accusations against him. Satan claimed that the only reason Job was such a goody-two-shoes was because God had made life so easy for him. Satan said that if Job had to experience any real trial or adversity, Job would prove to be just as ungrateful as all the other miserable malcontents that populated the earth. Despite Satan's accusations, Job proved to be a righteous soul.

Paul alludes to Satan as our accuser in Rom 8:33–34. Paul, however, triumphantly asserts that since Jesus is our defender— our defense attorney—our case has already been won. Whatever crime Satan may accuse us of, Christ himself has already paid the penalty; therefore, no one, and nothing, can now separate us from the love of Jesus Christ. We belong to him, and he will hold us securely in his hand.

I suspect that our enemy takes special pleasure when his lies and slander succeed in causing divisions within the body of Christ. For in such cases, his tactics not only deprive one of Christ's followers of peace, but two or more. Furthermore, by dividing us from one another, Satan is able to bring the church into disrepute and, in doing so, mock the name of Jesus. What better way to undermine the gospel of peace before the watching world than to stir up internecine strife among those who preach it? Fortunately for us, our God is patient and loving beyond measure, and despite our frailties and shortcomings, he is merciful with us even when our behavior causes his name to be dishonored.

When Satan's lies and accusations fail to achieve their desired end, our enemy will turn to other means in his effort to deprive us of peace and bring us to misery. We can see this, for example, if we return to the story of Job. In his efforts to shake Job's faith and to prove that Job was unworthy of God's love, the accuser caused a whole series of disasters to befall Job and his family. Similarly, when Satan failed to seduce Jesus with his temptations, he then resorted to violence. He convinced the religious and secular authorities—who normally were sworn enemies of one another—to collaborate in the brutal murder of Jesus. So, we must not dismiss the idea that our enemy could use violence, attacks on our health, attacks on our families, and so forth in the course of the spiritual struggle in which we are engaged. Jesus, in fact, tells us that if we are faithful in following him, we should expect to face this kind of opposition.

In Eph 6:11–19, Paul tells us that, given the spiritual nature of the war we are waging, we must not neglect to put on our spiritual armor. We must protect our hearts with righteousness—not with our own righteousness, for that is worthless. Rather, we must clothe ourselves in the righteousness of Jesus Christ. We must gird ourselves with truth—the truth that God loves us with a boundless, eternal love, and that nothing can separate us from that love. Our minds must be protected with the knowledge and assurance of our salvation—salvation not based on our own good works, but based on the sacrifice that Jesus made on our behalf. We need the protection of faith, and we need to know the word of God. In order to stand our ground, or even to press forward on the offensive, we need to be shod with the gospel of peace. Moreover, we need to pray. As Paul tells us, we must pray at all times.

How is the enemy attacking us today? What kind of lies has the deceiver whispered into your soul? What accusations has he brought against you? In what ways has he tried to sow divisions between us? What lies and accusations has he whispered about others? Has he used our pride to make us think we are better than the others, or have we believed the slander he has whispered against them, or against us? What does Scripture say about Satan's lies and accusations? What does it say about the existence of divisions within the church, the body of Christ? What is the root cause of such divisions? What is the truth that will protect us from the enemy's lies and slander?

A Mighty Fortress
by
Martin Luther (1529)
Translated from the German by
Frederick H. Hedge

A mighty fortress is our God,
a bulwark never failing;
our helper he, amid the flood
of mortal ills prevailing.
For still our ancient foe
does seek to work us woe;
his craft and power are great,
and armed with cruel hate,
on earth is not his equal.

Did we in our own strength confide,
our striving would be losing,
were not the right Man on our side,
the Man of God's own choosing.
You ask who that may be?
Christ Jesus, it is he;
Lord Sabaoth his name,
from age to age the same;
and he must win the battle.

And though this world, with devils filled,
should threaten to undo us,
we will not fear, for God has willed
his truth to triumph through us.
The prince of darkness grim,
we tremble not for him;
his rage we can endure,
for lo! his doom is sure;
one little word shall fell him.

That Word above all earthly powers
no thanks to them abideth;
the Spirit and the gifts are ours
through him who with us sideth.
Let goods and kindred go,
this mortal life also;
the body they may kill:
God's truth abideth still;
his kingdom is forever!

3

What's Wrong with My Hearing?

On that day Jesus had gone out of the house and was sitting by the sea. And large crowds gathered to Him, so he got into a boat and sat down, and the whole crowd was standing on the beach.

And He told them many things in parables, saying, "Behold, the sower went out to sow; and as he sowed, some seeds fell beside the road, and the birds came and ate them up. Others fell on the rocky places, where they did not have much soil; and they sprang up immediately, because they had no depth of soil. But after the sun rose, they were scorched; and because they had no root, they withered away. Others fell among the thorns, and the thorns came up and choked them out. But others fell on the good soil and yielded a crop, some a hundred, some sixty, and some thirty times as much. **The one who has ears, let him hear."**

MATTHEW 13:1–9

ONE OF THE REASONS we often lack peace is because our hearing and vision are impaired—spiritually, that is. This is not a physical problem. This is not because our eardrums are failing to reverberate when stimulated by sound waves, nor is it because our optic nerves are failing to detect visible light. Rather, it is because we can't hear God's voice or see what he is doing in our lives. Consequently, we remain in the grip of our anxieties and fear, and we continue to stumble through this broken world making the same mistakes over and over again. Why is this?

Have you ever wondered why on several occasions Jesus admonished his listeners, "The one who has ears, let him hear"? It is a very strange statement. Most of us, after all, were born with two ears. So, who was Jesus speaking to? By my count, this peculiar expression occurs fifteen times in the New Testament,[1] and there are several other places in Scripture where similar words are used to urge us to hear what God is telling us. Since most, if not all, of Jesus's listeners in fact had ears, what did he mean when he issued this odd exhortation?

In order to understand what Jesus was telling his listeners (who we can presume all had ears), we need to back up a bit and look at the broader biblical context in which this statement was spoken. First of all, we need to understand what kind of relationship God desires to have with his people. Scripture makes it abundantly clear on numerous occasions that God is not interested in maintaining an impersonal legal or business relationship with us.

1. Matt 11:15; 13:9, 43; Mark 4:9, 23; Luke 8:8; 14:35; Rev 2:7, 11, 17, 29; 3:6, 13, 22; 13:9.

In 1 John 4, we are told that "God is love." God created us to love him and so that he could love us. Indeed, he loves us passionately, and he wants us to love him in return. He wants to be our "first love" (Rev 2:4).

In 1 John 2:15, we are told not to love the world or the things that are in the world. These things are temporary and have no lasting value. Our desire should be for God and not for the stuff of this world. One of Satan's great deceits is that possessing the things of this world will give us greater delight than knowing the one who actually created these things. So, the old liar lures us into a love affair with something, or someone, other than God. However, to love the world and the things that are in the world more than we love God is idolatry.

Susan Cyre, in her book *From Genesis to Revelation God Takes a Bride*, shows how both in the Old Testament and in the New Testament, the language that God uses when he enters into a relationship with his people is actually the language of a marriage covenant. For example, in Exod 6:7–8, God declares, "Then I will take you as My people, and I will be your God; and you shall know that I am the Lord your God, who brought you out from under the labors of the Egyptians. I will bring you to the land which I swore to give to Abraham, Isaac, and Jacob, and I will give it to you as a possession; I am the Lord." In fact, this is the language of an ancient marriage covenant. This follows the formula that a groom would recite when taking a woman to be his wife. He would vow to protect her, take her into his home (or tent) and provide for her. In other words, when God made this vow to Israel, he was betrothing himself to the people of Israel. He was taking them as his bride. From this, we should understand that God desires a close, intimate relationship with his people. God loves his people as a husband ought to love his wife, and he wants us to love him as a wife should love her husband. That is the kind of love and commitment that the Lord wants from us.

Often we think of idolatry as the worship of man-made images—statues that have been fashioned from metal or wood. It is true that worshiping such images is a form of idolatry. However, idolatry is much broader than this. Idolatry is loving something—anything—more than one loves God. Idolatry is emotional and spiritual unfaithfulness to God, and it is a most serious disease of the soul. If left untreated, it is always fatal.

God wants our hearts. He wants our "first love." He does not want to be wed to an unfaithful spouse. In the book of Malachi (the last book of the Old Testament), God tells the people of Israel how much he loves them. Yet, he says he has observed their idolatry—their spiritual unfaithfulness. They have not loved him faithfully as he has loved them. He then likens their idolatry to the breaking of a marriage vow. God says that the covenant that he made with them was one of "life and peace" (2:5). His desire was to give his people life and for them to live in peace; however, they broke their marriage covenant. In doing so, they chose death over life, and they chose strife over peace. To what extent have we done the same?

God takes our unfaithfulness very seriously. In fact, he likens Israel's unfaithfulness to spiritual prostitution. We see this in Ezek 16:1–34 and in Jer 3:1–14; 3:20; and 5:7. It is also made abundantly clear in the story of Hosea, in which Hosea's wife Gomer continually runs away from her husband and engages in harlotry. God tells Hosea that the people of Israel are just like Gomer. Time after time, they have engaged in spiritual harlotry, for again and again they have given their hearts and their affections to someone, or certain things, rather than to the Lord their God. They have worshiped the creation instead of their Creator.

In the New Testament, the apostle Paul echoes this sentiment in Rom 1:21–25, where he writes,

> For even though they knew God, they did not honor Him as God or give thanks, but they became futile in their reasonings, and their senseless hearts were darkened. Claiming to be wise, they became fools, and they exchanged the glory of the incorruptible God for an image in the form of corruptible mankind, of birds, four-footed animals, and crawling creatures. Therefore God gave them up to vile impurity in the lusts of their hearts, so that their bodies would be dishonored among them.

For they exchanged the truth of God for falsehood, and worshiped and served the creature rather than the Creator, who is blessed forever.

In several places, Scripture tells us that we become like the things that we love and worship. If we love and worship God, we become more like him. The fruit of the Holy Spirit becomes more evident in our lives. However, Ps 115:8 tells us that those who fashion idols for themselves and those who put their trust in these idols will become like that which they idolize. The prophet Hosea says something similar in Hos 9:10: "They came to Baal-peor and devoted themselves to shame, and they became as detestable as that which they loved."

So, in what ways do we become like the things that we worship? The writer of Ps 115 tells us in verses 4–8:

> Their idols are silver and gold,
> The work of human hands.
> They have mouths, but they cannot speak;
> They have eyes, but they cannot see;
> They have ears, but they cannot hear;
> They have noses, but they cannot smell;
> They have hands, but they cannot feel;
> They have feet, but they cannot walk;
> They cannot make a sound with their throat.
> Those who make them will become like them,
> Everyone who trusts in them.

The prophet Isaiah is no less blunt in his assessment of those that make and worship idols. In Isa 44:14–19, the prophet declares of the idol maker:

> He will cut cedars for himself, and he takes a holm-oak or another oak and lets it grow strong for himself among the trees of the forest. He plants a laurel tree, and the rain makes it grow. Then it becomes something for a person to burn, so he takes one of them and gets warm; he also makes a fire and bakes bread. He also makes a god and worships it; he makes it a carved image and bows down before it. Half of it he burns in the fire; over this half he eats meat, he roasts a roast, and is satisfied. He

also warms himself and says, "Aha! I am warm, I have seen the fire." Yet the rest of it he makes into a god, his carved image. He bows down before it and worships; he also prays to it and says, "Save me, for you are my god."

They do not know, nor do they understand, for He has smeared over their eyes so that they cannot see, and their hearts so that they cannot comprehend. No one remembers, nor is there knowledge or understanding to say, "I have burned half of it in the fire and also have baked bread over its coals. I roast meat and eat it. Then I make the rest of it into an abomination, I bow down before a block of wood!

Later, the prophet Jeremiah would issue a similar admonition to the people of Israel: "For the customs of the peoples are futile; for it is wood cut from the forest, the work of the hands of a craftsman with a cutting tool. They decorate the idol with silver and gold; they fasten it with nails and hammers so that it will not totter. They are like a scarecrow in a cucumber field, and they cannot speak; they must be carried, because they cannot walk! Do not fear them, for they can do no harm, nor can they do any good" (10:3–5).

As the writer of Ps 115 tells us, idols "have eyes, but they cannot see; they have ears, but they cannot hear" (vv. 5–6). The psalmist also tells us that we become like the things we worship. When we dedicate our lives to anything, or anyone, other than God, we become as spiritually deaf and blind as the object of our affections. So, those who love their work more than they love God will become workaholics. Those who are in love with power will become dictators, if allowed to do so. Sometimes they will become dictators over nations, but often they will simply be dictators in their office, or home, or whatever their sphere of influence might be. Those whose first love is material wealth will become materialists. Those who love themselves will become narcissists. Moreover, all those who love and worship anything in place of God will become as spiritually deaf and blind as these things that they love. They will become as deaf and as blind as their idols.

This brings us back to Jesus's admonition: "The one who has ears, let him hear" (Matt 13:9). Who doesn't have an ear? If we know the context in which Jesus was speaking, we know that it is the idolator, the one whose misplaced affection has led to spiritual blindness and spiritual deafness! God wants us to love him with all of our heart, mind, soul, and strength (Deut 6:5; Matt 22:37). He wants our first love.

If we love God, we will become more like him. We will grow in love, wisdom, righteousness, and peace. Others will see the fruit of the Holy Spirit in us. Yet, the Lord will not coerce us. He will not force us into a relationship we do not enter into of our own volition. He gives us the freedom to love him or to pursue other lovers. He warns us, however, that we will become like the things that we love. If we choose to direct our affections elsewhere, we will become spiritually deaf. So, let those who have ears—that is, those who love the Lord—hear what he has to say.

Where do your affections lie? What is it that controls your wants and actions? Can you hear what the Lord is saying to you? If not, look into your heart. What do you idolize? Has your idol given you peace in the depths of your heart, or do you find yourself controlled by your fears and mired in ceaseless strife at multiple levels? If peace continues to elude you, if you have an ear, listen to what Jesus would say to you.

No Other Name
by
Matthew T. Dickerson
On the album
Streams of Mercy

We will give You thanks, we will lift up our praise
You are worthy of glory for all of Your ways
We offer You honor, Your works we proclaim
Salvation is found in no other name, in no other name

We give You our sorrow, we let flow our tears
We give You our heartache, our weakness, our fears
We give You our failures, we give You our shame
Comfort is found in no other name, in no other name

No other name in Heaven, no other name on Earth
Can offer the life that comes with rebirth
No other name below, no other name above
Fills our lives with the heights and depths of Your love
No other name

We come to You broken, we come in our need
We let go of our chains. By You we are freed
We come as the wounded, the weak, and the lame
For healing is found in no other name, in no other name

4

Mammon

No servant can serve two masters; for either [a person] will hate the one and love the other, or [else] be devoted to one and despise the other. You cannot serve God and [Mammon]."

Now the Pharisees, who were lovers of money, were listening to all these things and were ridiculing Him [Jesus].

LUKE 16:13–14

OF ALL THE DIFFERENT forms of idolatry, there is one that seems to attract the largest number of worshipers. This is the worship of Mammon. It is not surprising, therefore, that Jesus singled out this particular form of idolatry for special attention. In the text above, Jesus warned that you cannot serve both God and Mammon. You must choose one or the other. As denizens of the twenty-first century, we might wonder who, or what, Mammon is, and who serves this Mammon? Given that most of us have never heard of Mammon, how is this warning relevant to us?

Some modern English versions of the Bible make this a little clearer for us by translating "Mammon" as "wealth" or "riches." Jesus certainly had wealth and riches in mind here, so that is not necessarily a bad translation. However, Jesus's choice of the word "Mammon" was intentional and suggests yet a deeper layer of meaning that begs further exploration. Under normal circumstances, Jesus would have spoken in Aramaic, the common language of Palestine at that time. We can assume Jesus spoke in Aramaic in this instance. When Luke recorded the incident, he wrote in the dialect of Greek that was common at that time. Both Aramaic and Greek had other words for wealth and riches that Jesus (and Luke) could have used; however, Jesus intentionally chose to use the word "Mammon." Why?

It turns out that Mammon was the name of the Syrian god of riches.[1] That is, it was the name of a well-known idol. Hence, when Jesus told his listeners that they had to choose between serving God and serving wealth, Jesus was indicating that material possessions could become an idol. Luke informs us that the Pharisees were "lovers of money." Nevertheless, they considered themselves fine, morally upstanding keepers of the law. They clearly understood the point Jesus was making, and they must have been shocked, if not indignant, by the implication that they were idol worshippers. In fact, Luke tells us that they scoffed at Jesus's words.

Wealth, in and of itself, is neither good nor bad. As Paul told Timothy, it is the *love* of money that is the root of all sorts of evil (1 Tim 6:10). The Pharisees, who Luke tells us were lovers of money, were deaf to this suggestion. They believed that as long as they kept the letter of the law, it did not matter what unhealthy affections lurked within the recesses of their hearts. Jesus, however, made it clear that matters of the heart were of the utmost importance. Here, Jesus let it be known that people can, in fact, give their hearts

1. Wikipedia, "Mammon," para. 3.

to wealth instead of to God. The gift can replace the Giver as the object of one's worship and adoration. This was a point Jesus made very clearly in Matt 6:21 (another time when Jesus used the word "Mammon" for riches) when he said, "For where your treasure is, there your heart will be also." Do you trust in God to provide your daily needs, or is your sense of security based on the possessions that you own (or that own you)? Are you carrying on a love affair with Mammon, or is God your first and true love?

Idols, of course, have many limitations. The most obvious is that they are not living. They are deaf, dumb, and blind. As we saw in the previous chapter, Ps 115:4–8 tells us,

> Their idols are silver and gold,
> The work of man's hands.
> They have mouths, but they cannot speak;
> They have eyes, but they cannot see;
> They have ears, but they cannot hear;
> They have noses, but they cannot smell;
> They have hands, but they cannot feel;
> They have feet, but they cannot walk;
> They cannot make a sound with their throat.
> Those who make them will become like them,
> Everyone who trusts in them.

Those who put their trust in idols will be disappointed on the day of trouble, for they will find that their idols cannot save them. Moreover, idols can never give peace—shalom—to the soul. The hearts of those who put their trust in idols—such as Mammon—will remain troubled, insecure, and afraid. Our hearts will only find rest when they come to rest in God; for wealth and riches, although they may look tempting to the eye, cannot satisfy our deepest spiritual longings. In the end, Mammon will leave us wanting. It is like spiritual cotton candy. It is beautiful to look at—pink and sugary—and one assumes it will assuage one's hunger, but it melts away in an instant and leaves one with a longing for real nourishment.

There are many whose lips say that they trust in God, but whose actions reveal they have actually put their trust in, and given their hearts to, Mammon. Sometimes we don't realize that we have become followers of Mammon until the day of trouble arrives. Fortunately, Scripture offers a diagnostic test that will reveal where our affections actually do lie so that we can know the truth before that day comes—that is, if we really want to know the truth. Some people prefer to remain in ignorance.

In the book of Malachi (the last book in the Old Testament), God speaks to his people, and he says,

> "From the days of your fathers you have turned away from My statutes and have not kept them. Return to Me, and I will return to you," says the Lord of armies. "But you say, 'How shall we return?'
>
> "Will anyone rob God? Yet you are robbing Me! But you say, 'How have we robbed You?' In tithes and offerings. You are cursed with a curse, for you are robbing Me, the entire nation of you! Bring the whole tithe into the storehouse, so that there may be food in My house, and put Me to the test now in this," says the Lord of armies, "if I do not open for you the windows of heaven and pour out for you a blessing until it overflows. Then I will rebuke the devourer for you, so that it will not destroy the fruit of your ground; nor will your vine in the field prove fruitless to you," says the Lord of armies. "All the nations will call you blessed, for you will be a delightful land," says the Lord of armies. (Mal 3:7–12)

Earlier, God had commanded his people to give him the first tenth of everything that they produced or earned. This was known as their "tithe." The tithe was to be a sign that the people acknowledged that everything they had was a gift from the Lord and that they trusted the Lord to continue providing for them in the future. The tithe was evidence that the people had put their faith in God and not in Mammon. We will come back to this shortly. First, let me relate a short story I heard soon after I moved to Hungary.

Just after the Second World War, when Marxism was popular with many of the intellectuals, there was a farmer from a small village whose son went to Budapest to study economics at the big university. That fall, after this farmer had harvested his crops and things were slow on the farm, he decided to go to the capital to visit his son. When he got here, his son took him to hear a lecture by one of the new Marxist economists. The farmer was very impressed by what he heard, and when he went back to his village, he began to tell everyone how wonderful Marxism was.

One of his neighbors then started to question him about his new beliefs. The neighbor asked, "So how does this Marxism work?" The farmer said, "Well, according to the professor, if someone has two of something, and someone else doesn't have any, the person with two shares with the person who has nothing." His neighbor then asked, "Do you mean to tell me that, if you had two farms and I didn't have a farm, you would give me one of your farms?" The farmer replied, "That's right, if I had two farms and you didn't have a farm, I would give you one of mine." The neighbor went on to ask, "And if you had two plows and I didn't have one, you would give me one of your plows?" The farmer answered, "That's right! If I had two plows and you didn't have one, I would give you one of mine." The neighbor continued and asked, "And if you had two cows, and I didn't have a cow, you would give me one of yours?" There was a long pause. The neighbor asked again, "Well?" The farmer finally replied, "Now, that's not fair. You know I've got two cows."

The story is funny, but in some ways we often do the very same thing. We talk in theory about putting our faith in God, but when it actually comes to putting that faith into action, we object; we say, "That's not fair." Our belief is only in the abstract and does not affect what we do in practice in our everyday life. We say we trust in God, but, in fact, we trust in ourselves, or perhaps in Mammon.

Let me give you an example of what I mean. I may tell someone that I am a Christian. So the person asks me, "Do you mean to say that you believe that God exists?" I answer, "That's right, I believe God exists." The other person goes on to ask, "And you believe Jesus is his son?" "Yes, I believe Jesus is his son." The other person presses on and asks, "So you believe Jesus loves you, died for you, and offers you eternal life?" "Yes, yes, I believe all that."

"And God will take care of your every need?" I say, "Certainly!" And the other person asks, "So you trust God to the degree that you give him your tithe?" Then there is a pause. Finally, I say, "Wait a minute, that is too practical. That actually affects the way I live my daily life."

However, if we really believe down in the depths of our hearts that God exists, that he loves us, that his son died for our sins, that he offers us eternal life, and that he will take care of us, then our actions should reflect that faith. We should be willing to trust God with our tithe, and we should obey his commandment to give him the first fruits of all our labor.

Many of us, of course, have excuses why we don't do this. But, in fact, what it comes down to is that we don't believe God will really take care of us. Either that, or we are not sure God will give us what we want, so we try to do things our own way. As a result, we forfeit the peace God offers us.

Now you may ask, why does God want us to give our money to him anyway? Does he need the money? Will heaven go bankrupt without our tithes and offerings? No, that's not the reason. Is God a bitter old man who is trying to make our lives miserable? No! To the contrary, he loves us very, very much, and he wants us to experience true joy and peace. He wants to liberate us from the anxiety and fear that usually attend the followers of Mammon.

Also, just as God loves us, he wants us to love him. One of the reasons we give God our tithes and offerings is as a sign of our love for him. As Jesus said in Matt 6:21, your heart is where you put your treasure. What we do with our money reveals what is really in our hearts. If we truly believe in God and love God, if that is where our heart is, we will return to him a portion of the treasure he has given us.

Do you remember the story of the widow who brought her last two coins to the temple and offered them to the Lord? Jesus said that her offering was worth far more in the sight of God than all the gold and silver given by those who were rich. Why? Because this poor woman gave all that she had to the Lord, whereas the others gave from their surplus and from what they didn't need.

She loved the Lord. She also trusted him and put her welfare in his hands (Luke 21:1–4).

This leads to the second reason why God wants us to give our tithes and offerings to him. He wants to build our faith. He wants us to grow up and mature as believers. Faith only matures when it is put into practice and put to the test. Faith that is not put into action is only words—much like the old farmer's belief in Marxism. God is not an angry old man who wants to destroy our lives; rather, he is a generous and loving father who wants to bless us. However, we can only receive his blessings when our hands are open to receive them.

I remember when my children were younger how they would sometimes come across some worthless object but think this object was the most precious thing in the whole world. They would then hold onto it very, very tightly. One time, when my daughter was still a toddler, she found a piece of string. It was just a dirty, old piece of string she picked up off the floor somewhere, but she played with it and had all sorts of fun with it. She waved it in front of my face, but she would not let me take it away from her. The string wasn't even worth a penny. It was worthless. Abby, however, would not loosen her grip on it for anything, not even for a crisp, new hundred-dollar bill. That is because she was not yet mature enough to know what sort of things had lasting value.

We all do the same thing with God. He wants to bless us, but we can't accept his blessings because our hands are wrapped too tightly around the worthless things that we think are precious. We need to learn to trust God, to be willing to open up our hands and let go of our supposed treasures so that our Father in heaven can give us real treasures. If you really believe that God loves you and will take care of you, then trust him—trust him with your money. Open up your hands and give him the tithes and offerings he asks for.

Earlier we looked at Mal 3:7–12. Read it again! What does Scripture say here? It says that when the Israelites did not give God their tithe, they robbed him of what was his. Moreover, it says that they were cursed because of this. Think about all the people you know who spend so much time worrying about their financial situation. They never think they have enough, so they hold on to what they have with tight fists. In practice, they trust in Mammon and not in God. And what is the result? They are cursed with stress, ulcers, heart attacks, strokes, and the like. They think money will buy peace and contentment, but they experience the opposite. Instead of being able to buy peace, they find themselves beset by turmoil and anxiety.

In Mal 3:10, God tells us that when we learn to trust him, when we begin to give him the tithes and offerings that he wants from us, the curse will be removed, and he will "open for [us] the windows of heaven and pour out for [us] a blessing until it overflows." When we open up our hands to him and let go of the worldly treasures that we cling to, God will bless us—and he will bless us to the point that our blessings will overflow.

Some people interpret this to mean that God will make us wealthy. Televangelists twist Scripture in this way. They tell you that if you give your money to them, God will give more money to you. However, that is not what God promises! Sometimes his blessings do come in the form of material wealth, but most often his blessings take other forms. Yet, even if we are not rich in the world's eyes, we will not go hungry. God will always provide for us. Moreover, we will experience the blessing of peace and contentment, a blessing that money cannot buy.

Look at 2 Cor 9:6–13. Here Paul says that if you sow sparingly, you will reap sparingly, and he says this in the context of a discussion on giving and generosity. In other words, if you do not give, if you are not generous, if you do not trust God, you will not be able to receive much. You will be clutching your worthless piece of string so tightly that you will not be able to take hold of the gifts that your Father in heaven would give you. As a result, you will lose out on the blessings that you could enjoy. As Paul says in verse 8, "God is able to make all grace overflow to you, so that, always having all sufficiency in everything, you may have an abundance for every good deed." In other words, if we truly trust God and "sow" generously, not only will we always have sufficiency in everything, but we will also have an abundance for every good deed.

Did you catch the last part of that sentence? Paul says that God will give us an abundance . . . why? So that we might do good deeds! In verse 10, Paul says that God will supply us ("He who supplies seed to the sower") so that we can turn around and plant this seed, so that the seed can grow and produce a harvest of righteousness.

In the verse that follows, Paul tells us that as this happens we will be enriched, for not only will we supply the needs of the saints (our brothers and sisters and co-laborers in Christ) but—as he says in verse 13—through our obedience others will give glory to God.

Perhaps our bank accounts will not be enlarged, but we will grow rich in our hearts. We will have a joy and a peace within us that no amount of money can buy. Moreover, we will be free from the stress and worry that seem to rob people of their joy and even to kill off so many people before their time. This has been my own experience.

Let me bring this chapter to a close with a story I heard a few years ago. One of the old, prestigious universities in America decided to send out a questionnaire to all of its alumni asking about their careers, salaries, life styles, and financial status. The university wanted to confirm that its graduates went on in life to become wealthier and more powerful than those graduating from other schools.

One of the questionnaires made its way to an alumnus who was serving as a missionary in the midst of the jungle in South America. When he got it, he read it, chuckled, and filled it in. One of the questions asked whether the alumnus ever traveled abroad. That was an easy question to answer. He quickly checked yes and moved on. The next question asked whether the person ever traveled to exotic destinations. The missionary reckoned that the Amazonian rainforest counted as exotic. It was certainly full of exotic fruit and exotic wildlife. So again he marked yes. The following question asked whether the alumnus owned more than one home. In fact, the missionary did. Since he split his time between two separate villages which lay about a half-day's walk from one another, the natives in each village had built a hut for him to stay in while he was with them. So, again he marked yes. The questionnaire went on to ask whether the former student owned a boat. The missionary looked down toward the river where he saw his canoe lying on the bank. The natives had helped him fashion the canoe by hollowing out a tree trunk. Clearly, this was a boat of some sort, so once again, he said yes.

He continued filling out the questionnaire and found that on question after question he had to give answers which made it appear that he was a man of substantial means. Finally, he came to the end of the questionnaire, where he was asked to write down his annual earnings. He knew that the people back home would laugh at how little he made, so he laughed too and put down his salary. Then he said, "This will probably cause their computer to crash!"

According to the world's standard, this man was about as poor as he could be. Yet, he was happy and at peace. In his heart, he was a rich man. He had learned to trust God—to really trust God—to take care of him. So he was rich in God's blessings. And this is what God wants to teach us. God wants to teach us to trust him, not just with our words, but with our actions. God wants to teach us to open up our hands and to let go of the worthless trinkets we are clutching so that we might receive the gifts of great value he wants to give us—so that we can then use these gifts to enrich others.

Do you believe in God? Do you really believe that he loves you and will take care of you? Then stop putting your trust in Mammon. Instead, put your money where your mouth is. Give God your tithe and offerings. For if you do this, you will find yourself showered with his blessings—blessings the world may not always count as wealth, but blessings that will bring a depth of joy and peace that you have not experienced up until now.

Take My Life, And Let It Be
by
Frances R. Havergal (1874)

Take my life and let it be
consecrated, Lord, to thee.
Take my moments and my days;
let them flow in endless praise,
let them flow in endless praise.

Take my hands and let them move
at the impulse of thy love.
Take my feet and let them be
swift and beautiful for thee,
swift and beautiful for thee.

Take my voice and let me sing
always, only, for my King.
Take my lips and let them be
filled with messages from thee,
filled with messages from thee.

Take my silver and my gold;
not a mite would I withhold.
Take my intellect and use
every power as thou shalt choose,
every power as thou shalt choose.

Take my will and make it thine;
it shall be no longer mine.
Take my heart it is thine own;
it shall be thy royal throne,
it shall be thy royal throne.

Take my love; my Lord, I pour
at thy feet its treasure store.
Take myself, and I will be
ever, only, all for thee,
ever, only, all for thee.

5

The Extravagant

And He [Jesus] said, "A man had two sons. The younger of them said to his father, 'Father, give me the share of the estate that is coming to me.' And so, he divided his wealth between them. And not many days later, the younger son gathered everything together and went on a journey to a distant country, and there he squandered his estate in wild living. Now when he had spent everything, a severe famine occurred in that country, and he began doing without. So he went and hired himself out to one of the citizens of that country, and he sent him into his fields to feed pigs. And he longed to have his fill of the carob pods that the pigs were eating, and no one was giving him anything. But when he came to his senses, he said, 'How many of my father's hired laborers have more than enough bread, but I am dying here from hunger! I will set out and go to my father, and will say to him, "Father, I have sinned against heaven, and in your sight; I am no longer worthy to be called your son; treat me as one of your hired laborers."' So he set out and came to his father. But when he was still a long way off, his father saw him and felt compassion for him, and ran and embraced him and kissed him. And the son said to him, 'Father, I have sinned against heaven and in your sight; I am no longer worthy to be called your son.' But the father said to his slaves, 'Quickly bring out the best robe and put it on him, and put a ring on his finger and sandals on his feet; and bring the fattened calf, slaughter it, and let's eat and celebrate; for this son of mine was dead and has come to life again; he was lost and has been found.' And they began to celebrate."

LUKE 15:11-24

HIS FATHER WAS WEALTHY—THE wealthiest man in town. His estate sprawled over more acres than the younger son had ever cared to explore. There were fields of grain, as well as of vegetables. Orchards bore an assortment of fruit that was always plentiful in the kitchen, and the vineyards produced the best wine in the region. Then there was the livestock. The young man had no idea how many head there were of any of the animals. He only knew that they all stunk. He wanted nothing to do with their bleating and mooing or with the stench of their manure. He just wanted to get out of there as soon as possible. The estate may have been vast, but it was ever so boring. And there were always those chores to do—those dreadful chores—peppered, of course, with his father's continuous words of wisdom about the benefits of perseverance and enjoying the fruit of one's labor. How old-fashioned! He felt like a slave trapped on the most onerous of all slave galleys. He desperately wanted his freedom. He wanted to live his life extravagantly and to have fun and adventure. Instead, he was stuck here shoveling cow manure to the tune of his father's annoying aphorisms.

So, he came up with a plan. It was a gamble, but it might work. He decided to ask his father for his inheritance early. Why waste his youth waiting around for his father to die? After all, someday it would be his fortune anyway. He had a right to it. Why not get it now? His friends told him he was crazy. "Your old man will never go for that," they warned. One friend said, "My dad would be so furious. He would probably ground me for life. I am pretty sure he would disown me."

Nevertheless, starving for his freedom, the young man summoned up his courage and made his plea. He laid out a case why he should receive his inheritance now rather than later. He concluded his argument by imploring, "Father, give me the share of the estate that falls to me while I am still young and can enjoy it. Let me be free and live my life the way I want to live it."

The young man's friends were stunned when they heard that his father had agreed to grant this request. "What? He said he would give you your inheritance now and that you could go freely? He didn't quote any of the old laws or traditions? He didn't ground you . . . or worse, disinherit you?" The son was thrilled and immediately started making plans for his escape. He was too preoccupied with his dreams of an extravagant future to notice the pain in his father's eyes.

Nevertheless, the father was true to his word. His steward and accountant helped him assess the current value of the estate and figure out the younger son's share. In order to come up with the cash, the father sold off some of his livestock. He then handed the boy his share of the estate. It was an enormous amount of money. The son had never seen so much cash in all his life, and he couldn't get his hands on it fast enough. He quickly grabbed it with hands sweaty from excitement, and he hastily began to pack up his belongings. By the end of the week, he was on the road. When he left, he practically ran out the door and didn't even turn around to say goodbye.

When news of the young son's behavior started to spread, people were shocked. "That is outrageous! I've never heard of anything so disrespectful! A son—a younger son at that—asking for his inheritance while his father is still alive! The absolute nerve!" They were sure the father now considered his younger son to be dead to him. They could never understand why the old man sat in an upper window and stared off into the distance night after night. They reckoned the shock of the boy's inconsiderate, ungracious, and rude behavior must have led to some kind of early-onset dementia. Some whispered, "The old man's gone mad."

Now that the young man had his fortune in his hand, he was determined to live life to the fullest. No more boredom and drudgery. Instead, he was going to do what *he* wanted to do. He was going to be extravagant and was going to sample every delight that Mammon had to offer. That night, he spent a small fortune at a five-star restaurant he had heard about. With his dessert, he ordered the most expensive bottle of wine the establishment had in its cellar. Afterward, he paid a young woman to spend the night with him. He had never experienced so much pleasure in all his life. And this was just the beginning! His days of trudging around in animal dung were over, for now he was free.

The next day, he purchased a first-class ticket to Babylon—the city of cities. He had heard that in Babylon a person could enjoy every pleasure known to man, and he intended to sample them all. Upon his arrival, he was extravagant indeed. In fact, his extravagance quickly became legendary, and it didn't take long before he found himself surrounded by a cadre of new friends. His money flowed freely as they all immersed themselves, mostly at his expense, in Babylon's fast and furious social life.

However, his wealth, as sizeable as it was, had finite limits. In time, he managed to burn through most of the money his father had given him. His new friends took note when he started to become a little less extravagant and began to display symptoms of frugality and fiscal restraint. Instead of ordering the most expensive food and drink on the menu, he began to ask for the daily special. He also started counting every shekel he spent. His friends didn't think he was as much fun as he used to be, and they started drifting away. The women who used to flock to his bed could no longer be persuaded to spend the night with him—not for free, not when he wasn't extravagant. By the time his money ran out, he was all alone.

That happened to be the same time the economy went into a deep recession. Energy prices soared. A global famine made food scarce and very expensive. He hadn't worked a day since he had left his father's estate, but now hunger forced him to look for a job. Jobs, however, were hard to find in this depressed economy. At first, he had illusions that as the progeny of a man of great means some multinational corporation would be happy to give him a well-paid managerial position with generous benefits. That didn't happen.

He started looking for work at the top of the economic food chain, but rejection after rejection forced him to modify his expectations. Eventually, he worked his way down to the bottom of the barrel. In the end, he couldn't even get a minimum-wage job at the kebab stand on the street corner. He was turned away there, as well. Finally, a swineherd offered to provide him with very basic room and board in exchange for feeding his pigs.

"Pigs! Those foul, disgusting beasts. My father never raised pigs. They're unclean, and he didn't want those nasty animals anywhere near his farm. He said civilized people didn't touch those foul creatures. But look at me! Here I am slopping these vile animals for some uncouth barbarian . . . and I am so hungry . . . my insides ache . . . I would eat this revolting pig slop myself, if given half a chance.

"What has my life come to? My father's servants live better than this. I wonder . . . would my father take me back as a servant? What if I humbled myself, groveled before him, and confessed what a wretched son I am? But to be honest, I wouldn't take me back if I were he. I'm a worthless jerk. And the scandal . . . the people in town would show no mercy if I ever set foot there again. I would forever be the object of their scorn—and rightly so . . . but I am so hungry. Who would ever take back a no-good wretch like me? But what other choice do I have?"

One evening, as the father was sitting in the upper window gazing off into the distance, he saw a most forlorn figure trudging slowly down the road in the direction of his estate. He squinted. Is that . . . ? No, he is so filthy and bedraggled! Yet, could it be . . . ? He stared and tried to focus his old eyes. After a few more moments, he shouted, "It's him! He's alive!"

The old man quickly scrambled down the stairs as quickly as his old bones would allow. He shouted some commands to his servants. Then, in an action very unbecoming to a distinguished elder of the community, especially one of great means, he gathered up his robe between his legs and galloped down the road toward the dusty figure. It would be an understatement to say that he looked ridiculous. His servants stood there with their mouths agape. They had never seen their master behave so foolishly or with such a complete lack of decorum. What did all this mean?

When the father reached his son, the young man tried to say something. He tried to apologize. He tried to tell his father that he was a wretch and an unworthy son. He tried to ask for a position as a farmhand or simply as a servant. But he never got the words out correctly, for his father threw himself on his son and embraced him and kissed him. The father called to his dumbfounded servants, "Quickly bring out the best robe and put it on him, and put the family signet ring on his finger and sandals on his feet; and bring the fattened calf, slaughter it, and let's eat and celebrate; for this son of mine was dead and has come to life again; he was lost and has been found." So extravagant was his father's love!

****

So extravagant is *our* Father's love!

****

Psalm 103:10–14

He has not dealt with us according to our sins,
Nor rewarded us according to our guilty deeds.
For as high as the heavens are above the earth,
So great is His mercy toward those who fear Him.
As far as the east is from the west,
So far has He removed our wrongdoings from us.
Just as a father has compassion on his children,
So the Lord has compassion on those who fear Him.
For He Himself knows our form;
He is mindful that we are nothing but dust.

6

Mary and Martha

Now as they were traveling along, He [Jesus] entered a village; and a woman named Martha welcomed Him into her home. And she had a sister called Mary, who was also seated at the Lord's feet, and was listening to His word. But Martha was distracted with all her preparations; and she came up to Him and said, "Lord, do You not care that my sister has left me to do the serving by myself? Then tell her to help me." But the Lord answered and said to her, "Martha, Martha, you are worried and distracted by many things; but only one thing is necessary; for Mary has chosen the good part, which shall not be taken away from her."

LUKE 10:38–42

SCRIPTURE TELLS US THAT the first and greatest commandment is to love the Lord God with all of our heart, mind, soul, and strength. We can read this in Deut 6:5. Later, Jesus confirms the primacy of this commandment in Matt 22:37 and Mark 12:30. This commandment tells us why we were created. We were created to love God and to be in a right relationship with him. This is why we exist.

Saint Augustine opened his great work *Confessions* by saying,

> Man is one of your creatures, Lord, and it is his nature to praise You. He bears upon himself the mark of death, the sign of his own sin, to remind him that You stand against the proud. Nevertheless, since he is part of Your creation, his desire is to praise You. The thought of You stirs him so deeply that he can not be at peace unless he praises You. For You made us for Yourself, and our hearts will not find peace until they rest in You.[1]

The English word "Sabbath" is derived from the Hebrew word "Shabbath," which means to rest from labor. As Saint Augustine confessed, the need for Sabbath—rest from our labor—is built into creation. Members of the human race need Sabbath, as does creation as a whole. One of the purposes of Sabbath is to allow us the opportunity to draw near to God and learn to rest in him.

All too often, those of us who have grown up in the West forget this. We think our measure as human beings is based on what we do rather than on who we are. So, we go, go, go. We don't think we can afford to stop and rest for fear that we might not

1. Augustine, *Confessions* 1.1.

accomplish all that we should or could. Often we even think our measure as Christians is based on the good works that we do. We forget that we cannot continue to pour ourselves out unless we are constantly being refilled. If we do not make a place for Sabbath in our lives, we will run dry physically, emotionally, and spiritually. This is true of all of us—even those in full-time ministry. Eventually, we will come to the point where we will be unable to give any more, and we will burn ourselves out.

We think we will find peace if we achieve certain aims. To achieve these aims, we feel pressure to do more, accomplish more, earn more money, or win more acclaim. However, this is just another lie spewed forth by the father of lies. This is not why we were created, nor is it how we were meant to live. We forget that we were created to love and to be loved. Moreover, we were created with a need for rest. We forget, too, that the thing God wants most from us is not our labor, but us. God wants to spend time with us! He wants us to rest in him.

We get a little glimpse of this in Luke 10:38–42. Here we read that while Jesus was traveling along, he stopped to visit his friends Martha and Mary. Martha welcomed Jesus and his sizeable entourage into their home and immediately went to work preparing a meal for the large and hungry crowd. Meanwhile, Mary sat down by Jesus's feet and listened attentively to what he was saying.

Luke tells us that Martha then became distracted by much service. It often happens that when we are stressed out by the pressures of life; we lose patience with the people around us. This is what Martha did. She became upset with her sister. In fact, she was so upset that she complained to Jesus. She wanted him to tell Mary to quit sitting around and to get to work helping her serve. After all, Martha was engaged in very important ministry. She was attending to the needs of the Lord and his followers. What could be more important than waiting on Christ and his disciples? Martha was doing a fine work indeed! However, this was a big job. There were many hungry mouths to feed, and she needed assistance. Meanwhile, Mary, instead of helping Martha meet her important and urgent ministry goals, was just sitting around listening to

Jesus. So Martha came up to Jesus and said, "Lord, do You not care that my sister has left me to do the serving by myself? Then tell her to help me."

To me, that seems like a very reasonable request given the urgency and magnitude of Martha's task. If I had been in her shoes, I probably would have lodged the same plea. (I often think I know what other people should be doing with their lives!) Jesus, however, didn't respond in the way Martha was expecting. Instead, he gently reproved her: "Martha, Martha, you are worried and distracted by many things; but only one thing is necessary; for Mary has chosen the good part, which shall not be taken away from her."

Here we can see that from a divine perspective our service and deeds may all be very noble; nevertheless, we need to spend some time sitting at the feet of Jesus and listening to his words. In fact, sitting at the feet of Jesus might even be more important than serving him and his disciples dinner on time. Listening to Jesus is the "good part."

In the world in which we live, finding time to listen to Jesus will not happen by accident. There will always be some urgent task calling for our attention, but we cannot let what is urgent crowd out what is truly good. We must make room in our lives to rest in, and wait upon, the Lord. If we do not learn to rest in him, we will not find peace on this earth. Instead, like Martha, we will constantly find ourselves distracted. Very likely, we will even become grumpy and short-tempered. In that case, even if we are engaged in important and meaningful service, folks might tend to shy away from us. As a result, our testimony will not be the most effective.

This does not mean we should all quit our jobs and join a monastic community so that we can spend every waking hour in Bible study, prayer, and contemplation. Jesus does not tell us to withdraw from the world. In fact, there are many texts in Scripture that tell us it is good for us to work. Indeed, as followers of Christ, we have been given a specific mission to carry out. (We will look at this mission a little later on.) Scripture, however, also tells us that we need rest. After God created the world in six days, he himself rested on the seventh. He then told us that we are also to rest every seventh day—and we are to rest in him.

As a father, and now as a grandfather, one of the greatest joys I have experienced has been to have one of my young children or grandchildren fall asleep in my arms. I can remember several occasions when one of my offspring (or offspring's offspring) was fidgety, perhaps upset about something or not feeling quite right, and I lay down on the sofa and held the child close to my chest. The child resisted and squirmed for several moments—often letting out a few cries in protest—but eventually burrowed down between my neck and my shoulder and fell into a deep and restful sleep. It is a wonderful feeling to know that your child trusts you and feels safe in your arms. I strongly suspect that our heavenly Father also very much enjoys it when we, his children, bury ourselves in him and then fall into a state of deep rest and peace in his arms.

As the prophet Isaiah wrote, "Those who wait for the Lord will gain new strength; they will mount up with wings like eagles, they will run and not get tired, they will walk and not become weary" (40:31). In this same vein, Jesus, in Matt 11:28–29, said to those who would follow him, "Come to Me, all you who are weary and burdened, and I will give you rest. Take My yoke upon you and learn from Me, for I am gentle and humble in heart, and you will find rest for your souls."

My wife and I have found this to be true in our own lives. We set aside one day out of seven to rest and to enjoy the presence of God. We also carve out time each day to read Scripture, pray, meditate, and to listen to God. I do this in the morning because years of teaching early morning classes have made me into something of an early bird. I also find that this practice helps me get ready to face the challenges of the day with a greater degree of calm. My wife has her quiet time in the evening because she is more of a night owl. God has created each of us with a different rhythm. However, he has created all of us with a deep need to rest in him. If you have yet to experience this rest, or the kind of peace and strength that the prophet Isaiah spoke of, try setting aside time each day and one day each week to rest in the Lord. Sit at the feet of Jesus and listen to what he says. And don't be afraid to bury yourself in the presence of our heavenly Father and to find rest and peace in his embrace.

Thou Hidden Source of Calm Repose
by
Charles Wesley (1749)

Thou hidden source of calm repose,
Thou all-sufficient love divine,
my help and refuge from my foes,
secure I am, if Thou art mine;
from sin and grief and shame I hide me,
Jesus, in Thy name.

Thy mighty name salvation is,
and keeps my happy soul above;
comfort it brings, and pow'r and peace,
and joy and everlasting love;
to me, with Thy dear name, are giv'n
pardon and holiness and heav'n.

Jesus, my all in all Thou art;
my rest in toil, my ease in pain,
the healing of my broken heart,
in war my peace, in loss my gain,
my smile beneath the tyrant's frown,
in shame my glory and my crown.

In want my plentiful supply,
in weakness my almighty pow'r,
in bonds my perfect liberty,
my light in Satan's darkest hour,
my help and stay whene'er call,
my life in death, my heav'n, my all.

7

Matthew the Tax Collector
and Simon the Zealot

NOWADAYS, OUR SOCIETY IS more deeply divided than it has been at any time in recent memory. I suspect this observation doesn't come as a news flash. It seems we are suffering from a partisan

56

bipolar disorder in which all those standing anywhere to the right of center are labeled fascists and all those to the left are branded socialists. We hear a lot of name calling, but not much thoughtful discussion between those who hold divergent viewpoints. Much heat is being generated, but not much light. We stick labels on people who don't look and think like the members of the group we belong to. Once we have labelled these people, we then lump them together with everyone else who has been tagged with the same label. This makes it very easy for us to dismiss as irrelevant, or worse, all those belonging to said group. We tend to see stereotypes rather than individual human beings who were created in the image of God, and much of what we do and say is being driven by anger or by fear.

Unfortunately, many of the so-called news organizations are doing their best to stoke this anger and fear because this is how they bolster their ratings and generate more clicks on their websites. "News"—both on television and on the internet—has become a multibillion-dollar industry, and the marketing of fear is how these businesses generate more profit for their parent corporations. Politicians are also known to fan the flames of fear and anger as a means of building a loyal and passionate support base and of raising funds for their next election campaign.

What do you think Jesus would make of all this discord and anger if he were here today? In his own day, Jesus was known as a rabbi (or religious teacher), but he was a very unusual one. He didn't fit the traditional mold. For one thing, he didn't have a building or a physical location where he conducted his classes. Rather, he spent most of his time walking from place to place, and as he walked he taught. Furthermore, his students didn't choose him; rather, he chose his students. He picked those he wanted as his disciples.

We know that Jesus had a lot of followers and that some of these people were closer to him than others. On at least one occasion, Jesus sent seventy of his followers out on a mission. Then he had three, Peter, James, and John, who comprised his closest, innermost circle. For the most part, however, he spent his time with the twelve—a number that signifies the wholeness of God's kingdom. Prior to his crucifixion and resurrection, these men were referred to as his disciples—his students. After his resurrection and ascension into heaven, they were known as his apostles—those he had sent, or those who were on a mission.

It is obvious that when Jesus selected the twelve he had not read any handbooks on modern business and leadership theory or on church-growth strategy. Even if he had, I suspect he would have ignored their counsel, which strongly recommends that you choose people for your leadership team who are like-minded and who share the same vision. Jesus clearly did not do this. There is much that we do not know about the twelve, but we can surmise that Matthew the tax collector and Simon the Zealot represented the opposite poles of the contemporary culture wars.

Matthew, or Levi as he was also known, was a tax collector. Tax collectors worked for Rome. In fact, they didn't just work for Rome, they willingly collaborated with their overlords, and they usually did so in a way that allowed them to enrich themselves at the expense of their fellow countrymen. Rome would inform local authorities how much each district had to contribute to the imperial coffers. The local authorities would then put out a tender for tax collectors. These authorities were looking for people who would guarantee they could meet Rome's revenue quota. Anything the tax collector could extract from the local population over and above what was required of them they were allowed to keep for themselves. If someone won such a tender, the person would be assigned a military detail to make sure the tax collector was not roughed up or killed and to ensure that the empire got what it required from the district populace. It was expected that tax collectors would use their armed detail to shake down the people for as much as they thought they could bleed out of them. If done well, the job could be very lucrative.

In general, tax collectors were hated. They were the worst of the worst sinners. Not only were they willingly working for the enemy, but they were enriching themselves at the expense of their compatriots. In the local lingo, the Jews had a special category for tax collectors. They spoke of "sinners" and "tax collectors" separately, as if tax collectors were too rotten to be included with the regular, run-of-the-mill sinners.

You would think that if Jesus were trying to build a national movement to make Israel great again, he would not have invited a person like Matthew to serve on his strategic leadership team. Imagine the bad publicity Matthew's presence among his disciples would generate! Indeed, Jesus was often criticized precisely because he associated with tax collectors. For example, we can read in Matt 9:9–11,

> As Jesus went on from there, He saw a man called Matthew sitting in the tax collector's office; and He said to him, "Follow Me!" And he got up and followed Him.
> Then it happened that as Jesus was reclining at the table in the house, behold, many tax collectors and sinners came and began dining with Jesus and His disciples. And when the Pharisees saw this, they said to His disciples, "Why is your Teacher eating with the tax collectors and sinners?"

We don't know much about Matthew, but he is believed to be the author of the Gospel of Matthew. As a tax collector, he would have been highly literate and would have had the ability to write in Greek and possibly in Latin. He is mentioned as being present at the ascension of Jesus and therefore was an eyewitness to the resurrection. After Jesus returned to heaven, it is believed that Matthew preached the gospel in Judea until persecution caused him to flee. According to tradition, he was martyred for his faith in Ethiopia.

Given the fact that Jesus invited a collaborator with Rome to join his inner circle, it is interesting that he also called Simon the Zealot to join his leadership team. The Zealots were sworn enemies of the Roman Empire. Their goal—in fact their *raison d'être*—was to liberate Judea from Roman rule. They fully expected that Jewish independence would come only by means of a violent uprising. They were known to vent their wrath, often brutally, against Jews who collaborated with Rome. Their targets included tax collectors when given a chance.

Simon the Zealot is mentioned four times in the New Testament (Matt 10:4; Mark 3:18; Luke 6:15; and Acts 1:13). These are simply places where the names of the twelve are listed. Except for the fact that he was listed with the other disciples in these four texts, we know very little about him.

In Matt 10:4 and Mark 3:18, the Gospel writers refer to him as Simon the *Kananaios* or *Kananites*. Both *Kananaios* and *Kananites* are words that are sometimes mistranslated as "Canaanite." However, these two words are actually Greek derivations of the Hebrew word *qanai*, which means "zealous." So, a good English translation of these two verses should read "Simon the zealous" rather than "Simon the Canaanite."[1]

One wonders if at some point during his ministry Jesus gave Simon a new name, just as he had Simon Peter. Perhaps Jesus did the same with Matthew the tax collector, calling him Matthew—which means "gift of God"—instead of Levi?

When Simon joined Jesus's band of disciples, he was indeed a Zealot—that is, a political zealot. We can imagine, however, that as he studied at the feet of Jesus, he must have become more zealous for the kingdom of God. Perhaps at one point Jesus looked at Simon and said, "From now on you will be Simon the zealous instead of Simon the Zealot?" According to tradition, Simon was martyred in Persia when he refused to worship the sun god.

We know that at times there was some dissension between the disciples. For example, during the Last Supper when the disciples were expecting Jesus to expel the Romans and to restore the kingdom of David, they had a little argument among themselves over who would be the greatest in the kingdom of God.

One wonders if there was any noticeable tension between Matthew and Simon during the early days of Jesus's ministry. How did these two disciples at opposite ends of the political spectrum get along?

1. Wikipedia, "Simon the Zealot," para. 4. See also Nelson, "Who Was Simon the Zealot."

In any case we can assume that Simon's outlook and priori-
ties changed and matured as he spent time with Jesus. It is doubtful
that when Jesus first called him, Simon would have been thrilled
to hear his master say, "pay to Caesar the things that are Caesar's"
(Matt 22:21). I can easily imagine the new disciple spitting out
the wine that Jesus had just made from water if he had heard his
teacher utter such a treasonous statement. In the end, however,
if the stories of his death in Persia are true, Simon was willing to
give his very life for Christ. It is interesting that this man who had
once dedicated himself to restoring the political entity known as
the kingdom of David ended up dying on foreign soil for the sake
of the kingdom of God—a kingdom that Jesus made very clear was
not of this world.

In 2 Cor 5:17–19, Paul writes, "Therefore if anyone is in
Christ, this person is a new creation; the old things passed away;
behold, new things have come. Now all these things are from God,
who reconciled us to Himself through Christ and gave us the ministry of reconciliation, namely, that God was in Christ reconciling the world to Himself, not counting their wrongdoings against
them, and He has committed to us the word of reconciliation."

In Matthew and Simon, we see a good example of just what
this "word of reconciliation" looks like in practice. Jesus did not
allow himself to be dragged into the partisan battles of his day. Instead, he called both a collaborator with Rome and a sworn enemy
of Rome to come and follow him. Jesus then spent the next three
years walking and talking with these men. Over time, he lifted
their vision above the current political horizon and its partisan
fray and focused it instead on God. As these men spent time with
Jesus listening to his word, they were given a new perspective, a
heavenly perspective. They came to see that the kingdom of God
is not bound to any one secular political movement. It is much,
much bigger.

Jesus began by reconciling these two men to God the Father,
and as they became reconciled to God, they became reconciled to
one another. They became brothers in Christ. In the end, to the
best of our knowledge, both Matthew and Simon died in foreign

lands, not because of their allegiance to a political agenda, but because of their allegiance to Christ.

Paul tells us that first, God reconciled us to himself through Christ. Then, once we were reconciled to God, he called us to join in this ministry of reconciliation. As Paul says, he has given us "the word of reconciliation." We should ask ourselves, therefore, whether we see ourselves more as peacemakers and agents of reconciliation, or as judges, or perhaps as cultural warriors who would use the apparatus of secular power to impose a kind of superficial conformity to God's law? I wonder how often we forfeit the peace that God would give us because we immerse ourselves in the political and cultural wars of our day instead of serving as ministers of reconciliation? How often have God's people chosen to fight the wrong battles using the wrong strategies and the wrong weapons?

Just before Jesus began his public ministry, Satan tempted him with three temptations. One of these temptations was the offer to give Jesus all the kingdoms of the world. If only the ills of this broken world could be cured by means of political power! It would have been so much easier for Jesus to wear a secular crown and to fix all of our problems with the apparatus of government than it would have been to wear that crown of thorns. Think of the good he could have done as king of all the lands on earth. But Jesus knew that secular kings and politicians cannot cure what ails the human race; for our disease is a disease of the heart and soul. Rules that govern our outward behavior do not have the power to mend the soul, and trying to heal this broken world by forcing conformity to an external moral code is the spiritual equivalent of trying to heal cancer by applying a bandage.

You may recall that this was the approach taken by the Pharisees. They constructed a system of social and moral regulations. They then taught that if one conformed one's outward behavior to their rules, a person would be considered good and righteous regardless of any moral rot that might dwell within the soul. Jesus challenged this notion. In fact, he called these religious leaders whitewashed tombs (Matt 23:27). They were beautiful on the outside—like polished white marble—but inside there was the stench of death and decay. These self-appointed guardians of morality didn't appreciate this challenge to their authority. They felt threatened by this unorthodox rabbi. Consequently, they urged the Roman authorities to eliminate the threat. They aligned the powers of church (or temple) and state, and they crucified Jesus. However, this use of secular power to achieve religious ends didn't work out the way they thought it would. In fact, it worked out rather badly—as it invariably does.

Jesus knew that to heal the soul of man—to reconcile us to God and to save us from death—he had to go to the cross. So, he turned down Satan's offer of political power. How often since then has the church succumbed to Satan's temptation and attempted to wield the scepter of secular power—and in the process entered into very unholy alliances in the belief that by making such compromises it could achieve good things? Yet, with what result? If you are a fan of J. R. R. Tolkien and *The Lord of the Rings*, think of Boromir and his belief that he could use the ring of power for good.[2]

Paul tells us that Jesus pursued a ministry of reconciliation. We can see what this ministry looked like if we consider Matthew the tax collector and Simon the Zealot. Given that Jesus entrusted us with this same ministry of reconciliation, what should this ministry look like in your own life and in the life of our congregations?

2. Tolkien, *Fellowship of the Ring*, 413–16.

Blest Be the Tie That Binds
by
John Fawcett (1782)

Blest be the tie that binds
our hearts in Christian love;
the fellowship of kindred minds
is like to that above.

Before our Father's throne
we pour our ardent prayers;
our fears, our hopes, our aims are one,
our comforts and our cares.

We share our mutual woes,
our mutual burdens bear,
and often for each other flows
the sympathizing tear.

When we are called to part,
it gives us inward pain;
but we shall still be joined in heart,
and hope to meet again.

This glorious hope revives
our courage by the way;
while each in expectation lives
and waits to see the day.

From sorrow, toil, and pain,
and sin, we shall be free;
and perfect love and friendship reign
through all eternity.

8

Friendly Fire

WAR IS NEVER GOOD, and it always begets an abundance of tragedy. One of the greater of these tragedies is when the casualties of war are victims of friendly fire—that is, when people are killed or wounded by members of their own forces. Most often, the casualties are accidental. Sometimes they are not.

The same is true in the spiritual war in which we are engaged. Too frequently, those who claim to be followers of Christ are wounded by friendly fire. Sometimes this fire is accidental. Sometimes it is not. In either case, it is tragic, and in most cases it could have been avoided. The only one who benefits from the wounds we cause each other is Satan, our spiritual enemy.

We say we want to be at peace in our lives. True peace begins when we are at peace with God. Christ gives us this peace when we accept his forgiveness and entrust our lives to him. However, we cannot remain at peace with God without making peace with one another. Peace with God and peace with our neighbor are inextricably intertwined. Too often we forget this, and we sacrifice peace with God by clinging to our grudges and refusing to forgive our neighbor.

In Matt 18:21–35, Jesus tells us a story about a king who decided to settle accounts with his servants. While examining his ledgers, the king noticed that one of his servants owed him ten thousand talents. I have seen different estimates of what that might be equivalent to nowadays. Suffice it to say, it was a debt well beyond what any normal person, much less a lowly servant, would ever have been able to satisfy. Since it was obvious the servant would never have the means to repay this massive debt, his lord commanded that he, his wife, and his children be sold into slavery. Moreover, all the debtor's possessions were to be liquidated and whatever money was raised from these sales was to be used to repay some small portion of the total debt.

The servant, however, fell down before the king and begged for mercy. He said, "Have patience with me, and I will repay you everything" (v. 26). The king knew very well that this man would never be able to repay such a large debt; nevertheless, he had mercy. He showed compassion, forgave the servant's debt, and set him free.

So, what did the servant do then? No sooner had this man been spared a lifetime of slavery, than he went out and found one of his fellow servants who owed him a hundred denarii. A denarius would be about what you could earn in one day at a minimum-wage job. In other words, even though a hundred denarii would have been a significant sum of money to a servant, it was a negligible amount when compared to ten thousand talents. The first servant, however, filled with self-righteous indignation, seized the second and began choking him saying, "Pay back what you owe!" (v. 28). The second servant then begged for mercy: "Have patience with me, and I will repay you" (v. 29). You may have noticed that these were the very same words the first servant employed when he had begged for mercy from the king. Now, however, he turned a deaf ear to this plea when it was directed at him. Instead, he threw the second servant in prison until the hundred-denarii debt was repaid in full.

When the king's other servants heard about this, they became very upset, and they told the king what had happened. Thereupon, the king summoned the unmerciful servant to a second audience, at which he used some rather strong language. He said, "You wicked servant, I forgave you all that debt because you pleaded with me. Should you not also have had mercy on your fellow servant, in the same way that I had mercy on you?" (vv. 32–33). The king then handed the unmerciful servant over to the torturers until his entire debt was repaid. Jesus ended this story by warning, "My heavenly Father will also do the same to you, if each of you does not forgive [your] brother from your heart" (v. 35).

Jesus makes it clear that each one of us is like that first servant who owed his lord ten thousand talents. As mentioned earlier, in the context of this story this was a debt so large that the servant had no hope of ever paying it all back. It is a debt so great that we find ourselves owing our Lord everything we have and everything we ever will have, and still being without hope of ever settling our account. However, we cry out and beg for mercy. Because we ask for mercy, our Lord forgives us; he releases us from our debt and sets us free. We then have the opportunity to live in peace.

But what happens next? No sooner does our Lord forgive our great debt and offer us peace, than we see someone who owes us a hundred denarii—a debt significant in our eyes, but a tiny fraction of the debt we had been liable of. Compared to the debt we had once incurred, this person's debt to us is negligible! Nevertheless, we decide to assume the role of judge. We pronounce the other person guilty and demand justice. We declare that this person must satisfy the whole of the debt owed to us down to the last penny.

Our Lord, however, calls us back. When we stand before him this time, he reminds us that we were also debtors. When we could not repay our debt to him, he had mercy on us. When we deserved judgment, he forgave us and offered us new life—a life of peace. So what have we done? We have gone out and picked a fight with someone who owed us a hundred denarii. "How dare you!" the king says, "How dare you! You say that you want justice? Very well, then, justice you shall have! To prison you shall go until you pay back your entire debt of ten thousand talents. That is justice."

Like the first servant, all of us have sinned against our king, and we have all incurred a debt so great that we will never be able to work it off. At the same time, others have sinned against us. Perhaps someone that you trusted, or put your faith in, lied to you or let you down in a time of need. Maybe a partner cheated on you. Perhaps you were wounded by someone in your family. It is possible that you were the victim of a random crime, or maybe you suffered because of someone's recklessness or thoughtless behavior. The fact is, we live in a broken world, and without doubt you have been wounded. That is part of life on this earth.

The question then is not whether you have been hurt; rather, it is how you are going to respond to the hurt. You have a choice. You can: (A) forgive the one who hurt you, engage in a ministry of reconciliation, and endeavor to make peace; or (B) continue to aggravate the wound, carry a grudge, and remain in a state of war. You can: (A) let go of your anger, give it to God, and allow him to be the judge; or (B) try to push God off his throne so that you can play judge. In this case, you can continue dwelling on how badly you were hurt and continue agitating your emotional wounds so that they do not heal properly. Scripture, however, warns against choosing option B. Option B means the prolongation of war and a lack of peace, not only with the one who offended you, but with God.

Before we look at what Scripture has to say about this, let us first consider what it means to forgive someone. Emotional and spiritual wounds are similar in many ways to physical wounds. The deeper and more traumatic the wound, the longer it takes to heal. Moreover, some wounds are so deep and so serious that they leave permanent scars. We are commanded to forgive, so we must. Sometimes, however, the wound is so severe that this can only be accomplished with God's help, and even then, it takes time and only happens by degrees.

I do not believe that when we forgive someone, we necessarily forget what that person did. Rather, we let go of our claim to sit in judgment over that person. We let God be the judge. We stop dwelling on the wounds we received in the past. Instead, we look forward to the future and do our best to get on with our lives. In some cases, it is easy to forget what happened. In other cases, it is nearly impossible. In cases like these, we can forgive, but we cannot erase the scars, nor can we undo all the damage that was done.

Imagine you are out shopping one day when some kindly old lady whom you have never seen before accidentally runs her shopping cart over your toe and says, "Sorry!" That deed is relatively easy to forgive and forget. However, if you are betrayed by a person to whom you have given your heart, that will require some time, especially if the other person is not particularly repentant. In that case, I am not sure you can—or even should—forget what that person did. In such instances, forgiveness may simply mean that you give up your claim to sit in judgment over the person, and then you do your best to move forward with your life, leaving the past behind. If the person is unrepentant, I do not know if there is anything more you can do. On the other hand, if the person does express remorse and actually asks for forgiveness, then you may give the person the opportunity to win back your trust. But I do not think the trust is necessarily given automatically. Forgiveness is not the same thing as the restoration of a relationship. Forgiveness is simply letting go of your claim to be the judge. It is letting God be the judge. Forgiveness must be given, but the other person needs to rebuild what was destroyed through spite or unfaithfulness. Forgiveness allows a new opportunity to put things right, but it doesn't pretend that nothing happened.

In the Bible, when we see Jesus forgive—for example, after his resurrection when he restored Peter, who had denied him three times (John 21:15–17)—there is usually regret and remorse on the part of the one who is forgiven. These people recognize their sin and have a desire to get right with God. At other times—for example, when Jesus was hanging on the cross and he looked at the soldiers and the crowd—he simply turned the unrepentant, or the unknowing, over to his Father: "Father, forgive them . . ." (Luke 23:34). But even when Jesus restored Peter, he said, "If you love me, then do the following . . ."

In Matt 7:1–5 (part of the Sermon on the Mount), Jesus said to his listeners, "Do not judge, so that you will not be judged. For in the way you judge, you will be judged; and by your standard of measure, it will be measured to you" (v. 1–2).

Sometimes, we try to convince ourselves that it really is okay for us to judge someone else. We rationalize that somehow our case is special and that our situation is unique in the history of the world. God just doesn't know how badly we were hurt on this occasion. But keep in mind that God the Father does know what it is like to rescue his chosen people from slavery only to have them turn their backs on him and worship idols. He knows what it is like to send messenger after messenger to these people in order to get them to return to him, only to have these messengers ignored, beaten, or worse. He knows what it is like to send his very own Son to call his people home, and then to watch as these people nail his beloved Son to a cross. Moreover, Jesus knows what it is like to be betrayed by a member of his inner circle—and to be betrayed with a kiss! He knows what it is like to have his closest friends abandon him in his hour of greatest need. He knows what it is like to be falsely accused, publicly mocked, and beaten for sins he did not commit. He knows what it is like to have nails driven through his hands and feet—nails that were driven by the force of *our* ten-thousand-talent debt! Jesus knows what it is like to hang on a cross until his broken body finally relinquishes his spirit. Jesus does know our pain. Keep in mind, too, that even as Jesus hung on the cross, an innocent victim of hate and violence, he still refused to take his Father's place on the throne of judgment. You may remember that one of the last things Jesus said on the cross was "Father, forgive them; for they do not know what they are doing" (Luke 23:34).

Jesus tells us that when we judge another person, God will judge us according to the same standard of judgment that we use to judge others. As you judge, so you will be judged. I think a lot of us read these words in the Bible, but we do not take them seriously. We try to comfort ourselves with the notion that God does not really mean what he says here. God, however, does not use words frivolously. He means what he says. When he speaks, universes come into existence.

If you need yet more proof that Jesus meant exactly what he said when he told his followers that they must forgive if they expected to be forgiven, and that they must be merciful if they hoped to be shown mercy, look again at the Lord's Prayer. You can find this in Matt 6:9–13. Look in particular at verse 12.

Here, Jesus tells us to direct our prayers to our heavenly Father and to ask him for forgiveness. I like that part of the prayer! However, Jesus then says that when we ask for forgiveness we are to ask God to "forgive us our debts," or our sins, to the extent that we have forgiven those who are indebted to us, or who have sinned against us. In other words, Jesus taught that we will be forgiven as we forgive. We will be judged as we judge.

As followers of Christ, we are not called to judge the world. That is God's responsibility. Rather, we are called to lead the world to the foot of the cross. Since we have been forgiven, we are called upon to forgive. Since Jesus humbled himself for us, we are called upon to humble ourselves for the sake of others. Now that we have experienced mercy, we are called on to show others just where it was that we found it. To do this, we must demonstrate mercy through our actions and speech.

Back in the Middle Ages, England and France fought a running war that began in 1337 and did not end until 1453. The war spanned 116 years and became known as the "Hundred Years' War." The war began when Charles IV, the king of France, died without a clear successor. Edward III, the king of England, was the nearest male relative. He was Charles's nephew. So he staked his claim to the throne. The French nobility, however, had no desire to serve an English king, so they gave the crown to Philip, Count of Valois.

The two sides went to war, and five generations of kings spanning two dynasties fought on and off for over a century. Eventually, neither side remembered, or even cared about, the original cause of the war. Nevertheless, neither nation would give up the fight. Both sides claimed they had right on their side and refused to relent. They continued to do battle until both England and France were exhausted and virtually bankrupt. Thousands died in this conflict, and both countries suffered great loss. This is a good illustration of what happens to us when we will not forgive. We remain locked in combat, unwilling to back down. We battle for victory at any cost. The other party has done us wrong, and we demand justice (as we see it). But instead of victory, our pride and stubbornness only lead to death and destruction.

Recent medical studies have shed some light on the high price we pay for our internecine conflicts. Research synopses published by well-respected institutions such as the Mayo Clinic and Johns Hopkins Medical School show that people who are unforgiving often:

- bring anger and bitterness into every other relationship and new experience;
- are so focused on past wrongs that they can't enjoy the present;
- become depressed or anxious;
- feel that their lives lack meaning or purpose; and
- lose the sense that they are connected with others and thus experience deep loneliness.[1]

On the other hand, the studies also show that when people let go of their grudges and bitterness, they typically experience improved physical and emotional health. Specifically, researchers have observed that forgiveness frequently leads to:

- healthier relationships;
- improved mental health and higher self-esteem;

1. Mayo Clinic, "Forgiveness," para. 9.

- less anxiety, stress, and hostility;
- lower blood pressure;
- fewer symptoms of depression;
- a stronger immune system; and
- improved cardiovascular health.[2]

Have you been wounded by friendly fire? Or are you guilty of firing on others? Are you harboring the seeds of bitterness? Is there some old wound that you are holding onto that you will not let go of? Is there anyone that you refuse to forgive? If so, you need to humble yourself before the Lord, and you need to let these things go before they consume you. You need to do whatever you can from your side of whatever divide you may be on to make things right. As Jesus said in the Sermon on the Mount, "Blessed are the merciful for they will receive mercy" (Matt 5:7). Be quick to forgive in the same manner that you wish to be forgiven.

In 1 Cor 13:5, Paul tells us that love "does not keep an account of a wrong suffered." If we claim to be followers of Christ, if we truly love and trust God, we must put this love into practice. That means we must bury our grudges before they bury us. If you want to be at peace, then you must be a peacemaker.

Psalm 133

Behold, how good and how pleasant it is
For brothers to live together in unity!
It is like the precious oil on the head,
Running down upon the beard,
As on Aaron's beard,
The oil which ran down upon the edge of his robes.
It is like the dew of Hermon
Coming down upon the mountains of Zion;
For the Lord commanded the blessing there—life forever.

2. Mayo Clinic, "Forgiveness," para. 6; see also Johns Hopkins Medicine, "Forgiveness."

9

The Fear Factor

The Lord is my shepherd,
I will not be in need.
He lets me lie down in green pastures;
He leads me beside quiet waters.
He restores my soul;
He guides me in the paths of righteousness
For the sake of His name.
Even though I walk through the valley of the shadow of death,
I fear no evil, for You are with me;
Your rod and Your staff, they comfort me.
You prepare a table before me in the presence of my enemies;
You have anointed my head with oil;
My cup overflows.

Certainly goodness and faithfulness will follow me all the days of
  my life,
And my dwelling will be in the house of the Lord forever.

PSALM 23

DAVID BEGINS Ps 23 by declaring, "The Lord is my shepherd." I
think it is interesting that King David, the man who brought down
Goliath with a slingshot, the king who is considered the paragon
of Israel's grandeur, likened himself to a sheep. As a young man,
David himself had been a shepherd. He knew from his personal
experience that sheep are not the most intelligent creatures in the
animal kingdom. They don't always make the wisest of decisions.
In fact, they are prone to wandering off, getting lost, and even finding themselves stuck in places from which they cannot extricate
themselves. Moreover, sheep are not particularly good at defend-
ing themselves from predators. Sheep need a shepherd. Once they
have a shepherd, sheep then need to follow where the shepherd
leads them. The shepherd leads, and the sheep follow.

So, if we find ourselves in a place in which we need to be
rescued, we might want to ask whether we were paying attention
to our shepherd. Is it possible we wandered off on our own, did
things our own way, and found ourselves in a sticky situation from
which we could not extricate ourselves? A good question to ask
is, as sheep, have we been listening to the voice of our shepherd?
If not, what changes do we need to make in our lives? Another
thing we need to think about is what distractions do we need to
remove from our lives? Have we been attentive to the voice of our
shepherd, or have we allowed the noise and the din of the world
around us to drown it out?

In John 10, Jesus tells us that he is the good shepherd. And
here in Ps 23, David tells us that he will make us lie down in green
pastures and will lead us beside quiet waters. These statements
merit further attention. First of all, if we are confident that we can
lie down, then we must know that we are safe. We can be sure our

shepherd will protect us, even when we are sleeping. Therefore, we need not be afraid. I will come back to this point shortly. Second, not only do we trust that our shepherd will protect us, we also have assurance that he is going to provide for our needs. Green pastures are good pastures. These are places where we can get the sustenance that we require. Moreover, I have read that sheep do not like to drink from swiftly moving water. For whatever reason, they seem spooked by water that has ripples and waves, and must be coaxed to drink from it. Some sheep simply will not drink from it at all, even if they are dying of thirst. They will choose to drink from dirty, polluted puddles instead.[1] Our shepherd knows this, and, if we trust and follow him, he will lead us to quiet water. He knows our quirks and eccentricities, as well as our weaknesses, and he will provide for our needs.

In verse 3, David says the Lord, his shepherd, restores his soul! The other place in Scripture where this choice of words is used is Ps 19:7, which says "The law of the Lord is perfect, restoring the soul." So, we can see that the restoration of the soul is somehow connected with a knowledge of the Lord and of his law, or word. It is interesting to note here that we do not restore ourselves. There are no magic rituals and no self-help exercises that will restore our soul. Bookstores are full of self-help books that tell you how *you* can restore your soul, but this is something only God can do. Spiritual disciplines are good and useful and have a proper role in our growth and maturity, but we should not imagine that we can restore our souls by mechanically carrying out any of these disciplines.[2]

We must remember that the Christian faith is not a set of rules that we must follow, nor is it a set of doctrines that we must believe, nor is it a checklist of things we must do. Rather, it is a personal relationship, and it is a relationship that is based on love.

1. Keller, *Shepherd Looks*, ch. 4; see also Schoenian, "Feeding and Watering," para. 8.

2. Richard Foster has said the spiritual disciplines "put us in a place where we can experience inner transformation as a gift." Foster, "Danger of Spiritual Disciplines," para. 3.

In the same way that you cannot fix other personal relationships through the mechanical performance of some specified actions on a checklist, you cannot draw close to the Lord just by *doing* certain things. The restoration of the soul is a matter of the heart. There is really only one thing that we can do to restore our souls. As Jer 29:13 tells us, "You will seek Me and find Me when you search for Me with all your heart." For the restoration of our souls, we must turn to our shepherd and seek him with all of our heart. This is where the work comes in any relationship. We must seek God with all our heart. To do this, we must study his word, we must spend time with him in prayer, and we must join others in worshiping him, because these are the primary ways in which he communicates with us.

David continues, "Even though I walk through the valley of the shadow of death, I fear no evil, for You are with me; Your rod and Your staff, they comfort me" (v. 4). Here, the "valley of the shadow of death" is a poetic way of referring to death. The ancient Hebrews believed that when a person died, that person's soul, or shadow, went to a place called Sheol. Sheol is something like a shadowland where the souls of the dead rest. There, disembodied spirits wait until they are raised to life on the day of judgment. So David was saying that even if he were to die, he need not fear death. In fact, in Ps 139:8, David says that even if he were to make his bed in Sheol, the Lord would be there with him. Knowing that the Lord, his shepherd, is watching over him with his rod and staff, David can sleep in peace—even in Sheol.

The key phrase in verse 4 is "I fear no evil," which can also be translated "I fear no harm." Since death is the greatest enemy of all, and since David says he doesn't have to fear death, David declares he does not need to fear any harm whatsoever. This is a most important statement! Psychologists have said and written much about how our fears play a major role in guiding our behavior. Some of this we know from our personal experience. For example, I remember how my eldest grandson, Max, used to get on his bike and hurl himself down his concrete driveway with total abandon. When he was young, he was fearless. However, after his face had

had a few close encounters with the pavement, he became a tad more circumspect. I have noticed that he now conducts a very careful risk analysis before attempting any new death-defying feat of daring. His experience has taught him to take a more cautious approach to his physical activities.

Many years ago, I lived in one of the more forlorn neighborhoods of Trenton, New Jersey. One day, while I was working on my front porch, a fellow who lived up the street—one who had fried too many of his brain cells on angel dust—sneaked up behind me and tried to take my head off with a stave he had ripped off another neighbor's fence. Later, he told the police that voices had told him to kill me. I survived the attack, but afterward I caught myself constantly looking over my shoulder to see what sort of malefactors might be lurking behind me. I had never done that before. Fear had changed my behavior. It had made me more defensive.

Fear does this at the emotional level, as well. When we have been hurt emotionally, we tend to put up defensive barriers in order to prevent the recurrence of similar pain. This is very obvious in children who have suffered severe trauma. We can see it, too, in those suffering from PTSD. But it is also something that happens to some degree even in seemingly normal, well-adjusted adults—like most of us. Once our souls have felt the pain of a relationship gone wrong, we tend to put up protective barriers so that we don't experience similar pain again. The problem with these defensive barriers is that they also prevent us from developing strong healthy relationships with others here in the present. As members of Christ's body, we are required to build these relationships with one another.

David tells us that we need not fear any evil, or any harm, for even death is powerless to hurt us. The Lord is our shepherd. His rod and his staff comfort us. So what do *you* fear? How have you been injured in the past? How have these wounds affected your behavior and your attitudes? What defensive barriers have you erected to prevent the recurrence of similar wounds?

Sometimes the pains we have experienced in the past give rise to fears, and these fears lead us to misinterpret the words and actions of others here in the present. Likewise, sometimes the pains others have experienced lead them to misinterpret our words and actions. So, sometimes we feel, or cause, pain even when there was no ill intention. We are simply reacting in fear because of some previous experience. But here is the thing: David goes on to tell us that even if those around us do have malevolent intentions, even if they really are trying to hurt us, we still do not have to be afraid. For the Lord will set a table for us to feast, even in the midst of our enemies. He will anoint our heads with oil. He will protect us and keep us safe. Goodness and mercy will follow us all the days of our lives, and in the end, we will dwell in the house of the Lord forever.

Given the fact that the Lord is our shepherd and his rod and his staff protect us, we need not fear. Not even death can separate us from the love of the Lord. Yet, we know that fear does, indeed, continue to play a role in our words and actions. Much of what we do and say is done to protect ourselves from the things and experiences that we fear. We need, therefore, to seek God with all our heart, but then we have to ask him to reveal our deepest fears to us. Let us ask God to help us identify those experiences in the past that have given rise to fear and to our defensive behavior. Then, once he has helped us to identify these fears, we can give these fears to our shepherd so that he can handle them. Let us also try to tune out the distractions in our lives so that we can better hear the voice of our shepherd. As we allow our shepherd to restore our souls, I think we will find that he will also restore many of the relationships that we have with those who live with us in this broken world.

Amazing Grace
by
John Newton (1779)

Amazing grace! how sweet the sound,
That saved a wretch like me!
I once was lost, but now am found,
Was blind, but now I see.

'Twas grace that taught my heart to fear,
And grace my fears relieved;
How precious did that grace appear
The hour I first believed!

The Lord hath promised good to me,
His word my hope secures;
He will my shield and portion be
As long as life endures.

When we've been there ten thousand years,
Bright shining as the sun,
We've no less days to sing God's praise
Than when we first begun.

10

Peace

"Comfort, comfort My people," says your God. "Speak kindly to Jerusalem; and call out to her, that her warfare has ended, that her guilt has been removed."

ISAIAH 40:1-2

WE LIVE IN A fallen and shattered world. It is a world that is at war on many different levels. This, however, is not what God intended for us. God meant for us to live in peace. It must be noted, however, that peace—true peace—is not contingent upon one's physical circumstances. Peace is not simply the outward cessation of hostility. It is not living under a temporary truce or cease fire. In fact, Jesus once told his disciples very specifically that he had not come to bring this sort of temporal tranquility (Matt 10:34). Indeed, he told his followers that they should actually expect rough treatment in this world if they chose to follow him. Yet, they were to be at peace in the midst of turmoil, even if suffering persecution.

Technically, North Korea and South Korea are still at war with each other. They agreed to a ceasefire approximately seventy years ago, but the state of war between the two Koreas has never formally come to an end. No peace treaty has ever been signed. As a result, today, tens of thousands of solders remain arrayed on both sides of the line that demarcates these two political entities. The soldiers from the two nations are separated by minefields and barbed wire, and they are armed and ready to begin shooting at a moment's notice. In fact, sometimes an overly anxious soldier does squeeze a trigger and the two sides exchange a burst of fire. While they may not be pursuing active military campaigns against one another at the moment, they are not at peace.

You probably know some people who are in relationships that are a lot like this. The two parties have entered into a ceasefire, but they are not enjoying true peace. Tensions remain high as both sides have erected defensive barriers and have laid minefields to protect themselves from anticipated incursions by the other party. Either side could open fire at any time, and every attempt at conversation is like trying to tiptoe through one of those minefields without setting off an explosion. Perhaps you yourself have experienced such a relationship? Or perhaps you are in such a relationship? If so, insofar as it depends on you, what can you do to end this state of war and to enter into peace?

We need to keep in mind that the Hebrew word for peace, "shalom," encompasses much more than the temporary cessation of hostilities between warring parties. It also includes the idea of wholeness, tranquility, and well-being.

The prophet Isaiah told us that when the Messiah came, he would make peace between God and creation. In so doing, he would also bless our souls with wholeness, tranquility, and well-being. He would do this first of all by taking away our iniquity and bearing it upon himself. He would remove the barrier, the curse of sin, that separates us from God, and he would bring genuine peace to the world. In Isa 40:1-2, the prophet proclaims, "'Comfort, comfort My people,' says your God. 'Speak kindly to Jerusalem; and call out to her, that her warfare has ended, that her guilt has been removed.'" Isaiah foretold of a time when Jerusalem's warfare would end and she would experience peace. She would experience peace because her guilt would be removed!

Isaiah 11:1-10 gives us a picture of what this peace will look like at the end of time when the Messiah returns and sets all things right:

> Then a shoot will spring from the stem of Jesse,
> And a Branch from his roots will bear fruit.
> The Spirit of the Lord will rest on Him,
> The spirit of wisdom and understanding,
> The spirit of counsel and strength,
> The spirit of knowledge and the fear of the Lord.
> And He will delight in the fear of the Lord,
> And He will not judge by what His eyes see,
> Nor make decisions by what His ears hear;
> But with righteousness He will judge the poor,
> And decide with fairness for the humble of the earth;
> And He will strike the earth with the rod of His mouth,
> And with the breath of His lips He will slay the wicked.
> Also righteousness will be the belt around His hips,
> And faithfulness the belt around His waist.
> And the wolf will dwell with the lamb,
> And the leopard will lie down with the young goat,
> And the calf and the young lion . . . will be together;
> And a little boy will lead them.
> Also the cow and the bear will graze,
> Their young will lie down together,

And the lion will eat straw like the ox.
The nursing child will play by the hole of the cobra,
And the weaned child will put his hand on the viper's
    den.
They will not hurt or destroy in all My holy mountain,
For the earth will be full of the knowledge of the Lord
As the waters cover the sea.
Then on that day
The nations will resort to the root of Jesse,
Who will stand as a signal flag for the peoples;
And His resting place will be glorious.

When the Lord returns and puts things right, Isaiah tells us that the wolf shall lie down with the lamb, and his resting place will be glorious. This is not what I see now when I watch the birds at my in-laws' bird feeder, but this is what God promises we will experience in his kingdom at the end of time. He intends for all creation to be at peace and to find rest in him.

On seven different occasions, New Testament writers refer to God the Father as the God of Peace.[1] God's Son, Jesus, is called the Prince of Peace (Isa 9:6), and one day he will rule from new Jerusalem. The name "Jerusalem" literally means "city of peace." Moreover, God promised that he would make a covenant of peace with his people (Isa 54:10). He also said on several occasions that he would bestow the gift, or blessing, of peace on those who follow him and who put their trust in him.[2] On this side of judgment day, our peace is only partial. We can have peace within our souls. After judgment day, however, all of creation will be at peace in every respect.

Have you accepted this gift of peace that God has offered, or are you still at war with God or with your neighbor? Saint Augustine once observed how young children will often cling to some worthless trinket because it is shiny or has an outward appearance that attracts their attention. They will wrap their little hands tightly around the object and refuse to let go—even when their parent

---

1. Rom 15:33; 16:20; 2 Cor 13:11; Phil 4:9; 1 Thess 5:23; 2 Thess 3:16; Heb 13:30.

2. Num 6:22–26; Ps 72:3–7; Isa 26:1–12; 48:18; 66:12.

offers a gift of surpassing value—and as long as their hands are clenched tightly around the trinket, they cannot accept a gift of far greater value from their parent. As mentioned earlier, I observed this tendency once when my daughter, at a young age, found a dirty piece of string and thought it was the most wonderful thing in the world. She wouldn't trade it to me for anything.

Are you clinging to something that is keeping you from accepting the gift of peace that God wants to give to you? Mammon? The desire for prestige or fame? Striving for position or authority? Anger or bitterness? Fear? Are you bearing a grudge against someone? Is there anything in your life that you need to let go of so that you can accept the surpassing gift of peace that our heavenly Father is offering to us?

When I was young, I had a great many fears. For one thing, I was terribly shy. As a result, I was afraid to speak in front of people that I did not know well. I had other fears, as well. When I was nine years old, my family moved from the city out to the country. Our new home was the only house on a dirt road, and it was surrounded by one hundred acres of woods. I was given a bedroom in the basement. I liked this room because it was the biggest bedroom in the house; however, I frequently imagined that wild animals were lurking outside my windows. Sometimes, I imagined that unsavory criminal types were out there, as well. So, when darkness fell, I became afraid. Sometimes, my fear kept me from enjoying a good night's rest. If I heard a noise outside my window, I would freeze. Like the squirrels in my in-laws backyard, I would lie there motionless like a statue as I peered into the darkness in an effort to detect any pending threats to my well-being. Then one night as I was getting ready for bed, I read Ps 27, which begins:

> The Lord is my light and my salvation; whom should I fear? The Lord is the defense of my life; whom should I dread? When evildoers came upon me to devour my flesh, my adversaries and my enemies, they stumbled and fell. If an army encamps against me, my heart will not fear; if war arises against me, in spite of this I am confident. (vv. 1–3)

It struck me that if God really did exist—and I believed he did—then I did not need to fear. Even if there were an army of malefactors outside my window, and even if an assortment of the scariest forest creatures were on the prowl around our house, God would protect me. I could be confident in him. So, I prayed. I gave my fears to God and asked him to guard and keep me. I also asked him for the faith I needed to trust in him for my safety. And suddenly, just like that, I found that I did believe. At the same time, I felt a lightness of heart. My fears vanished. I have more or less slept soundly ever since.

When God promises peace in this world, he is not promising the absence of war, nor is he promising the sort of conditional ceasefire we often see between warring parties. Rather, he is promising wholeness, tranquility, and a deep peace of soul. He is promising rest for the weary-hearted, for we know we can sleep while he stands guard over us. In Matt 11:28–29, Jesus calls to us, "Come to Me, all who are weary and burdened, and I will give you rest. Take My yoke upon you and learn from Me, for I am gentle and humble in heart, and you will find rest for your souls."

When Jesus promises peace, first and foremost he is promising the absence of fear. Have you ever noticed that when angels appear in the Bible, often the first thing they say is "Do not be afraid,"[3] a command that Jesus also gives to his followers on several occasions?[4] However, in order to enjoy this peace, we have to be willing to trust our lives to him, and we have to trust him with every aspect of our lives.

According to my count, on sixteen different occasions writers of New Testament epistles greeted their readers with a blessing along the lines of "Grace and peace be with you."[5] Why do you think they said this over and over? What did they mean by it? Sometimes we skim over these words without much thought,

3. Luke 1:13, 30; 2:10.

4. Matt 14:27; 17:7; 28:5; 28:10; Luke 5:10; 12:32; John 6:20; Rev 1:17.

5. Rom 1:7; 1 Cor 1:3; 2 Cor 1:2; Gal 1:3; Eph 1:2; Phil 1:2; Col 1:2; 1 Tim 1:2; 2 Tim 1:2; Titus 1:4; 1 Pet 1:2; 2 Pet 1:2; 2 John 1:3; 3 John 1:14; Jude 1:2; Rev 1:4.

telling ourselves that they are just some sort of ancient formulaic greeting. We then rush to get to the "substance" of the epistles. But maybe we need to meditate a bit more on why these particular words were included in God's word. How and why did this become a uniquely Christian blessing?

In the days leading up to his crucifixion, Jesus said to his disciples, "Peace I leave you, My peace I give you; not as the world gives, do I give to you. Do not let your hearts be troubled, nor fearful" (John 14:27). Then on two occasions when he appeared to his disciples after his resurrection, the very first thing he said was "Peace be to you" (Luke 24:36, John 20:19). Again, sometimes we gloss over these simple words as we rush to find some more profound lesson in the words that follow. We assume that Jesus was just repeating the words to some common greeting—a social nicety. However, as mentioned elsewhere, God does not use words frivolously or casually.

Nowadays, many postmodern intellectuals argue that words have no clear meaning. As a result, they say we cannot really communicate with one another with any degree of certainty, and they would deny the power both of blessings and of curses. However, God's words do have meaning, and his words have power. Jesus truly meant for us to be at peace in him, regardless of our circumstances. After all, when Jesus appeared to his disciples following his resurrection, he had just defeated death—the greatest enemy of all. If death no longer has any claim over our lives, what do we really have to fear? If God can vanquish death, surely we can also trust him to see us through all the lesser challenges of this life.

During these very strange days in which we live, when often it looks like the world has been plunged into chaos and violence, we need to keep in mind that this has actually been the norm ever since the fall. Sometimes I hear people saying, "The world is going to hell in a handbasket." However, the truth is that ever since Adam and Eve disobeyed God (Gen 3), this world has been under the authority of Satan, otherwise known as the "prince of the power of the air" (Eph 2:2). All of creation is now in a state of war. We have been separated from God, and creation is groaning under the curse of sin. Nevertheless, now that Jesus has paid the price for our sins, we can be adopted as children of God. We can dwell in his presence and live in peace!

Paul tells us in 2 Cor 5:18–19 that Christ came to reconcile the world to himself, and he has made a way for us to be reconciled to the Father. Not only that, but he has also called us to join him in this "ministry of reconciliation." Naturally, this is something that is hard for us to do if we are not yet at peace. This is almost impossible for us to do if we continue to live in fear behind defensive walls, or if we are not at peace with one another.

Are you at peace—truly at peace in the depths of your soul? Do you trust God fully and completely in all aspects of your life? Have you let him speak peace into your soul? If not, what fears still control you, and how do they effect your words and behavior?

It Is Well with My Soul
by
Horatio Spafford (1873)

When peace like a river attendeth my way,
when sorrows like sea billows roll;
whatever my lot, thou hast taught me to say,
"It is well, it is well with my soul."

> *It is well*
> *With my soul;*
> *It is well, it is well with my soul.*

Though Satan should buffet, though trials should come.
let this blest assurance control:
that Christ has regarded my helpless estate,
and has shed His own blood for my soul.

My sin oh, the bliss of this glorious thought!
my sin, not in part, but the whole,
is nailed to the cross, and I bear it no more;
praise the Lord, praise the Lord, O my soul!

O Lord, haste the day when my faith shall be sight,
the clouds be rolled back as a scroll;
the trump shall resound and the Lord shall descend;
even so, it is well with my soul.

11

I Feel the Earth Move
Under My Feet . . .

IT IS EASY TO complain. We all do it. Complaining is also contagious. As soon as one person gives voice to a complaint, others usually join in. In fact, we frequently find ourselves in subtle competitions to see who can spin the tale of greatest woe and who can lay claim to being the victim of the greatest injustice. We need to keep in mind, however, that fostering an attitude of disgruntlement is one of the stratagems our spiritual enemy employs to deprive us of peace. After all, it is hard to be at peace when one is chronically dissatisfied.

In the first place, grumblers are generally persuaded that the universe ought to revolve around them and cater to their wants and needs. When it doesn't, they give voice to their dissatisfaction, and the complaints pour forth.

We may say with our lips that we believe in God. However, our actions do not always reflect that faith. The faith that we profess does not always shape the way we think or live. It is not a living faith that forms and molds the core of our being. Rather, our outlook remains largely egocentric. The universe, we believe, ought to be more sensitive to our wants and needs. Our faith is not a passionate relationship with our first love. Rather, it is just sterile religion—a set of rules and regulations we imagine, if correctly followed, can be used to manipulate God.

When you love someone—truly love someone—you stop residing at the center of your own little universe. The other person's wants and needs become more important to you than your own, and your love for that person reorients the way in which you see the world. When God is our first love, our lives become centered on pleasing him.

There are those, however, whose faith is little more than words. It does not shape who they are. It is more of an add-on, or fashion accessory, to their egocentric existence. They pursue their affair with Mammon, or fame, or pleasure, or whatever, while they give lip service to God. Their version of Christianity is more of an eternal life insurance policy than a living relationship with their Creator and Redeemer. When the idols that they are serving fail to satisfy their wants and desires, which they inevitably do, they tend to blame God. So, they complain and grumble.

We have established that this world is a very broken place. It is a place ruled by the father of lies and a place where death currently has its way. Those who expect this world (and its idols) to fulfill their wants and needs will always end up disappointed. They will never find peace.

Not long ago, I was rereading the book of Numbers in the Old Testament. Chapter 16 of Numbers tells the story of Korah, Dathan, and Abiram. These men and their followers were chronic grumblers. They displayed a very self-centered attitude, and they seemed to be of the opinion that the universe should cater to their whims. The way they saw it, if they carried out the rituals that were required of their religion, God should put their needs and wants before all else. The universe should make them comfortable. One of the symptoms of this egocentric view of religion was serious memory loss.

These men had been present when God freed the Hebrews from slavery and then delivered them from the Egyptian army by making a way for them to cross the Red Sea—on dry land! They had witnessed firsthand how God had led them through the wilderness and had protected them with a pillar of fire. They had witnessed God providing the Israelites with food and water in the desert. They had witnessed all of these miracles and more. Nevertheless, they complained long and hard about Moses and Aaron and their leadership.

Their memory loss seemed to give rise to a distorted sense of nostalgia, for they painted a romantic version of how great life used to be back in Egypt when they could satisfy their gastronomical hankerings with leeks and onions and other tasty treats and when they didn't have to rely on God to provide them with manna. They forgot to mention the whole slavery experience and how the Pharaoh had sorely mistreated them. Instead, they complained that Moses and Aaron had led them out of the comfort they claimed they had enjoyed in Egypt and into the barren wilderness. They also complained that they had not inherited a land flowing with milk and honey as promised. (They neglected to mention that this delay in entering the promised land was due to their own unfaithfulness!) Anyway, as a result of their grumbling, the earth shook. In fact, the ground opened up beneath them and swallowed them and all that they possessed. Things didn't end well for these malcontents. So much for the power of grumbling.

There is another instance in the Bible when human words led to a major movement of the earth's crust. In Acts 16 we can read what happened when Paul and Silas were arrested in Philippi. First, they were beaten with rods, and then they were thrown into prison. To me, such treatment would constitute legitimate grounds for complaint. If I had been there, I probably would have led the grumbling. After all, Paul and Silas had been doing God's work! They had been spreading the gospel. However, instead of getting a pat on the back for a job well done, their reward was to be beaten up by local rabble-rousers and thrown into prison—a most dank, dark, unpleasant place to be! Furthermore, they were chained to the walls. Not only had their rights been violated, but they had been sorely mistreated. I am quite sure they experienced a high degree of physical discomfort that day. Surely this maltreatment in the course of their missionary service was legitimate cause to lodge a complaint with the Almighty. However, in Acts 16:25–26 we read, "Now about midnight Paul and Silas were praying and *singing hymns of praise* to God, and the prisoners were listening to them; and suddenly there was a great earthquake, so that the foundations of the prison were shaken; and immediately all the doors were opened, and everyone's chains were unfastened" (italics added).

Paul and Silas had been beaten with rods, locked in a dark prison, and chained to the wall . . . and they sang hymns of praise! Instead of focusing on whether their current desires were being met, or on whether they had been treated with the appropriate respect, they remembered the great things God had done in the past. For Paul and Silas, their faith in God was not ancillary to their lives, it formed the very core of their being. Their love for God shaped their character, and it shaped the way they viewed the universe. They did not suffer the illusion that the universe existed to satisfy their wants and needs. They knew very well that this world is a war zone. It is broken and under the curse of sin. So instead of complaining, they remembered what Christ had done for them on the cross. They remembered his goodness, mercy, and love. And despite the fact that they had been beaten and chained to a wall in a dark prison cell, they were at peace. So, there in the midst of that darkness, they sang about that goodness and love. As a result, the earth shook. Their chains fell off, and the prison doors swung open. Nevertheless, they remained in their cell and continued to sing praises to God. At the end of the story, the jailer himself became a follower of Christ and was baptized together with his whole household.

In both of the stories we just looked at, the earth quaked in response to the words people uttered. (Keep this in mind when you are tempted to think words don't matter!) In the first instance, the ground opened up and swallowed a group of grumbling malcontents. I am guessing that put an end to the complaining competition within the Israeli camp that day. In the second instance, an earthquake freed those who had been giving praise to God from the discomfort of a dark prison cell. Not only that, but their praise of God led to the liberation and salvation of several others.

In the King James translation of the Bible, Ps 22:3 says God "inhabitest the praises of Israel." The NASB says God is "enthroned upon the praises of Israel." Think about that for a moment. Somehow, and in some way, God inhabits, or dwells in, or is enthroned upon the praises of his people. When we praise the Lord, he shows up!

Do you want to shake the world? Do you want to set the captives free? If so, then give praise to God and thank him for his great goodness. In these weird days in which we live, it is easy to focus on the negative and to join the chorus of complainers. We should remember, however, that we have a spiritual enemy—one who hates it when we worship the Lord. He is constantly trying to turn our attention away from God and his great mercy. Instead, he wants us to turn inward and focus on ourselves and on our various problems and complaints. However, we must not let the enemy succeed in turning us into grumblers. Instead, we ought to sing hymns of praise to God. Let us shake the world with our praise so that others might be set free from their chains. In the process, we just might find that we are freed from our own fears and anxieties, and we might find true peace.[1]

1. As an interesting sidenote, more and more medical research is finding

O for a Thousand Tongues to Sing
by
Charles Wesley (1739)

O for a thousand tongues to sing
My great Redeemer's praise,
The glories of my God and King,
The triumphs of His grace.

My gracious Master and my God,
Assist me to proclaim,
To spread thru all the earth abroad
The honors of Thy name.

Jesus! the name that charms our fears,
That bids our sorrows cease,
'Tis music in the sinner's ears,
'Tis life and health and peace.

He breaks the pow'r of canceled sin,
He sets the pris'ner free,
His blood can make the foulest clean—
His blood availed for me.

Hear Him, ye deaf; His praise, ye dumb,
Your loosened tongues employ;
Ye blind, behold your Savior come,
And leap, ye lame, for joy.

Glory to God and praise and love
Be ever, ever giv'n
By saints below and saints above—
The Church in earth and heav'n.

---

evidence that a grateful attitude has numerous physical and emotional benefits. See, for example, Travers, "Expressing Gratitude."

12

Ambassadors, Judges, Warriors, and Spies

Therefore, we are ambassadors for Christ, as though God were making an appeal through us; we beg you on behalf of Christ, be reconciled to God.

2 CORINTHIANS 5:20

EARLIER, WE NOTED THAT Jesus has given us a mission. As much as he wants us to spend time with him on a regular basis, he does not want us to withdraw from the world. Indeed, he wants us to live out our faith in the very midst of this fallen world. If you are married, I hope you jealously guard the time you have with your spouse each day If you are not married but are in a serious relationship, I am sure you treasure every moment you are able to spend with your loved one. Nevertheless, as much as we may enjoy whiling away the hours in the company of those that we love, we know we have to go out and do our jobs most days of the week. Unless you are retired, you can't just sit home and admire the person of your dreams.

Keeping this in mind, let us examine a little more closely what Paul says about us being ambassadors of Christ. We know that this present world belongs to Satan. Therefore, we should not be surprised to find ourselves at war on multiple levels—from the international to the intrapersonal. However, in Col 1:13, Paul reminds us that God the Father has delivered us from the domain of darkness and has transferred us to the kingdom of his beloved Son—the Prince of Peace. In Phil 3:20, Paul then says that, as a result of this transfer, our citizenship is now in the kingdom of heaven. We are no longer citizens of this fallen realm in which we presently reside. This kingdom is no longer our home. We are living here as aliens; for now our citizenship is in God's kingdom. In 2 Cor 5:20, Paul goes a step further and declares that we are not merely citizens of God's kingdom, we are more than that—we are also his ambassadors! We have been given a mission. We are to represent Christ and his kingdom here on earth.

Over the years, I have taught the children of several diplomats. So, I have learned a bit about the special job that ambassadors have. Ambassadors are commissioned to represent their home country in the land where they are sent to serve. In our case, that means we are to represent Jesus Christ and his kingdom to the people living around us here in the domain of darkness. As we live in this dark and war-torn world, it is our job to represent the Prince of Peace. Or, as stated in the introduction, we are to be keepers of the light.

As part of our diplomatic assignment, we have been given the ministry of reconciliation. Sometimes we forget this and mistakenly labor under the illusion we have been called to serve as judges. However, Christ is the judge, and he will fulfill his juridical duties on judgment day. Our job is simply to let others see something of Christ and his kingdom through us. In the midst of the strife and warfare in which this world is engulfed, our job is to show others where they can find peace.

Another job we have not been given is that of warrior. Often, we get caught up in the rhetoric of the culture wars, and we imagine that we have been called to bring the pagans and heretics into some kind of outward submission to our moral code. Unfortunately, if we look at what is happening in Ukraine at the present time, we can see where this kind of rhetoric can lead.

Kirill, the current patriarch of the Russian Orthodox Church, has framed this war as a holy war in which "Christian" Russia must defeat the forces of a liberal and decadent West in order to restore the true Christian church. In this holy war, Kirill has dubbed Vladimir Putin the one chosen by God to make Russia (and its church) great again.[1] Moreover, in order to achieve this great "moral" victory for the "true" church, Kirill has justified murder, pillage, rape, and other atrocities. He has even sanctioned the destruction of churches and the execution of pastors and priests who are not loyal to the Russian Orthodox Church.[2] Kirill would use secular force to impose his version of Christian morality from the top down. We should keep in mind, too, that when Jesus's followers wanted to use force to overthrow the Roman authorities and to install Jesus as the king of Israel, he chose the way of the cross.

While some Christians see themselves as judges or warriors, others try to play the role of spy. They see themselves more as secret agents than as ambassadors. Instead of going out and being examples of salt and light to the world around us, they hide from the world in fear. They know the world is against us, so they go under cover and keep their identity as followers of Christ secret.

---

1. A good analysis and synopsis of Kirill's ideology and of the Russian version of the church-state synthesis can be found in Harned, "Holy Wars."

2. See, for example, Nelson, "Moscow Continues Targeting Christians."

In fact, according to research done by the Barna Group, "evangelical" Christians in North America are just about the most isolated group in American society![3] Studies done in Scotland and Germany suggest that this is true of evangelical Christians in Europe, as well.

By "isolated" Barna means that evangelicals, as a group, are the people least likely to have friends who differ from themselves or who hold different beliefs. Moreover, they tend to gather their information only from those sources that serve to reinforce their opinions. To a large degree, evangelicals talk to themselves and listen to themselves. According to Barna's findings, evangelicals are the group least likely to engage in a meaningful conversation with those who disagree with them on substantial issues. Practically speaking, they have retreated behind a series of defensive barriers and into their own subculture. Instead of seeking to transform society by means of a spiritual renewal of the heart, too often (like Kirill) they appeal to secular authorities to impose on society an external code of moral behavior. This, however, is not a strategy that has ever borne any real fruit. In fact, it is one that has consistently led to the weakening of the church and its witness.

As a result of this evangelical isolation, large sections of society are not hearing the good news. In fact, an increasing number of those born after 1985 have little or no contact with the church or with its ambassadors. When they do have contact with the church, too often they are not impressed. For the body of Christ has increasingly succumbed to temptation and compromised its role as ambassador of the kingdom of God by entangling itself in unholy political alliances.

Nowadays we see this same phenomenon occurring in Hungary, where I lived for over thirty years. The older historic churches have (unequally) yoked themselves to the party that is currently in power. They have done this with the hope of creating (they would say reestablishing) their particular version of a Christian Hungary—a version that they are trying to impose from without by means of legislation rather than from within through the

3. Barna, *Barna Trends 2017*, 112–15.

transformation of people's hearts. They are trying to use the force
of law to bring about an external conformity to their traditional
standard of morality. As a result, the younger generation is turning
away from organized Christianity in large numbers. I suspect that
in the coming years Hungary may witness a backlash resembling
the cultural revolution that America experienced in the 1960s.

Recent research has shown that approximately 72 percent
of the Hungarian population identifies itself as religious.[4] An
overwhelming percentage of these people identify themselves as
Christian! Yet, less than 10 percent of the population actually at-
tends worship services more than twice a year or is active in any
meaningful way in a congregation.[5] So, although a majority of
Hungarians claim to be followers of Christ, very few know what
that actually means or looks like in practice.

I could be wrong, but it seems to me that what is needed—
both in Hungary and in most countries throughout the West—is
for those of us who claim to be followers of Christ to do a better
job as ambassadors. So, how can we do that? I'll come back to this
question in a moment, but first let me digress a bit and tell you the
true stories of two very different diplomats.

The first is Raoul Wallenberg. Wallenberg was a Swedish
diplomat who served his country in Hungary during the later
stages of World War II. He is widely given credit for saving tens of
thousands of Jews after the Nazis seized control of the country in
March 1944. Wallenberg arrived in Budapest that July and served
until the Red Army arrived in December. During his brief tenure,
Wallenberg issued thousands of "protective passports" to Jews and
sheltered as many as he could in buildings that he declared were
under the protection of the Swedish embassy.

When Wallenberg took up his post in Budapest, the Nazi
campaign against the Jews of Hungary had already been under-
way for several months. During the three-month window between
May and July 1944, over four hundred thousand Jews had been

4. Sahgal and Cooperman, "Religious Belief," first graph. See also Luke,
"Faith, Politics, and Paradox," para. 5.

5. Sahgal and Cooperman, "2. Religious Commitment," para. 6 with graph.

packed into cattle cars and deported. The vast majority of these deportees had been sent to the Auschwitz-Birkenau concentration camp, where they were gassed and cremated. According to most estimates, only about 230,000 Jews were still left in Hungary at the time of Wallenberg's arrival. Wallenberg, however, hit the ground running and immediately went to work with Per Anger, another Swedish diplomat, issuing protective passports. These passports identified the bearers as Swedish citizens awaiting repatriation. Wallenberg then demanded the German authorities recognize those holding one of these protective passports as subjects of Sweden. As such, they were exempt from German law, including the law requiring Jews to wear yellow badges. Moreover, those holding such passports were spared deportation.

In addition to issuing these protective passports, Wallenberg used money at his disposal to rent thirty-two buildings in and around Budapest. He declared that these buildings were under the authority of the Swedish Embassy. Therefore, according to international law, the buildings were considered Swedish territory and were protected by diplomatic immunity. To reinforce his claim, he posted signs on these buildings identifying them as "The Swedish Library," "The Swedish Research Institute," and the like. He also hung large Swedish flags on the front of the buildings to let everyone know the buildings were under the protection of the Swedish government. Wallenberg used these buildings to provide shelter to almost ten thousand Jews.

One of Wallenberg's drivers, a man by the name of Ardai Sándor, recounted the action Wallenberg took one day when he intercepted a trainload of Jews that was about to leave for Auschwitz. Ardai wrote,

> He [Wallenberg] climbed up on the roof of the train and began handing protective passports through the doors which had not yet been sealed. He ignored orders from the Germans to get down, then the Arrow Cross [the Hungarian Nazis] men began shooting and shouting at him to go away. He ignored them and calmly continued putting passports into the hands of those who were

reaching out for them. I believe the Arrow Cross men deliberately aimed over his head, as not one shot hit him, which would have been impossible otherwise. I think this is what they did because they were so impressed by his courage. After Wallenberg had handed out the last of the passports he ordered all those who had one to leave the train and walk to the caravan of cars parked nearby, all of which were marked in Swedish colors. I don't remember exactly how many, but he saved dozens off that train, and the Germans and Arrow Cross were so dumbfounded they let him get away with it.[6]

So that is how Raoul Wallenberg used his position as a diplomat and how he used the resources at his disposal to save the lives of many who otherwise would have been sent to a certain death.

Then there is the story of Gueorgui Makharadze, a diplomat from the Republic of Georgia. At one time, Makharadze was the second-ranking diplomat at Georgia's embassy in Washington, DC. However, on January 3, 1997, after drinking prodigious amounts of alcohol, Makharadze got behind the wheel of his car and attempted to drive. In this impaired condition, he caused a five-car accident in which a teenage girl was killed and four other people were seriously injured. When he was later tested, authorities discovered that his blood alcohol content was still 0.15. The police, however, had to release him because he claimed diplomatic immunity and said he was not subject to the laws of the US. When the story of his misdeed became front-page news, his country was so embarrassed by his behavior that the president of Georgia revoked his diplomatic privileges and allowed him to stand trial in the US. Gueorgui Makharadze had not represented his country well. In fact, he had brought shame and embarrassment to the people of Georgia.

But let's return to the question of how we can do a better job as ambassadors of Christ. To begin with, if we are going to be ambassadors, we have to leave our gated communities, and we have to leave our defensive attitudes behind. We cannot serve as

6. Kunich and Lester, "Profile of a Leader," 96.

ambassadors if we are isolated from the world we have been sent to reach. Nor can we serve as effective ambassadors if we are acting like secret agents, warriors, or judges.

Several years ago, I taught two brothers whose father was a Hungarian diplomat. They told me that according to international law, an embassy is actually considered a little piece of the country that it represents. So, too, are the homes and vehicles used by diplomats. Therefore, when my students visited their father at the Hungarian embassy in Iran, they were actually standing on a little piece of Hungarian territory. The same was true when they were riding in their father's car and visiting his residence. That meant that Hungarian law was in effect in these places rather than the laws of Iran.

Have you ever thought of your home (or your car, or your office) as an embassy, as a little piece of the kingdom of heaven here on earth—as places where others might catch a glimpse of divine light? Have you ever thought of them as places where the law of grace and the law of love apply rather than the law of death? Or as places where your guests might find a few moments of peace and refuge from the wars in which they are engulfed? As an ambassador, do you actively open up your home to others? Or are you a secret agent who uses your home as a place to hide? Do you live as though you were an ambassador who is here to represent the Prince of Peace or do you behave more like a spy who is trying to complete your earthly assignment and get through this war without being caught? Or perhaps you prefer playing the role of judge or holy warrior?

Paul tells us that we are ambassadors for Christ. As diplomats, what kind of job are we doing representing our king and his kingdom? Are we using our resources to lead people from death to life as Raoul Wallenberg once did, or are we bringing shame and disrepute on the kingdom that we serve as the diplomat from Georgia did? Or are we simply working undercover as secret agents?

Not long ago, a former student of mine was given a post at the Hungarian consulate in New York City. She was part of the cultural delegation there. Her job was to help organize events that would let the people of America see a little slice of Hungarian culture. If we are ambassadors, then we should be using our resources to do something similar on behalf of the kingdom we represent. We should be using our homes, offices, vehicles, and so forth to give others a glimpse of heavenly culture.

If we are ambassadors, and not secret agents (or judges or warriors), we should also be making efforts to strike up new friendships with people who are different from us—and we should be praying for them! We should be engaging our neighbors, co-workers, classmates, and others in dialogue without sitting in judgment on them. Moreover, we should be looking for opportunities to invite them into our "embassies" to give them a glimpse of the kingdom that we represent.

Many of us look at ourselves and rightfully conclude that we are not gifted evangelists. That is okay! Not many of us are. But we can still invite people to events where the gospel is made known. We can invite people to church, to Bible studies, concerts, and the like.

Some people might argue that the people around us are sinners and unholy and that we ought to keep away from them. However, you may recall that Jesus chose to spend a significant amount of his time with those whom the "good" people of his day frowned upon—people the Pharisees said were unrighteous and unholy. Jesus hung out with tax collectors, prostitutes, Samaritans, and the like. In fact, he even called a tax collector to join the band of his disciples. Why did he do this? He did this because he came to reconcile people to God and to bring peace. What did the religious authorities have to say about this?

Finally, the most effective way that we can serve as ambassadors is to demonstrate Christ's love to one another and to the world. 1 John 4:12 tells us that "no one has ever seen God; if we love one another, God remains in us, and His love is perfected in us." In other words, no one has seen God face-to-face. However, when we love one another, God is present among us, and then the world can see something of God through us. This is how we can best do our jobs as ambassadors—by demonstrating the love of Christ before the watching world. Love is our most powerful apologetic.

Love Divine, All Loves Excelling
by
Charles Wesley (1747)

Love divine, all loves excelling,
Joy of Heav'n to Earth come down,
Fix in us thy humble dwelling,
All thy faithful mercies crown;
Jesus, thou art all compassion,
Pure, unbounded love thou art;
Visit us with thy salvation,
Enter ev'ry trembling heart.

Breathe, O breathe thy loving Spirit
Into ev'ry troubled breast;
Let us all in thee inherit,
Let us find thy promised rest;
Take away our love of sinning;
Alpha and Omega be;
End of faith as its beginning,
Set our hearts at liberty.

Come, Almighty to deliver;
Let us all thy grace receive;
Suddenly return, and never,
Never more thy temples leave.
Thee we would be always blessing,
Serve thee as thy host above,
Pray, and praise thee without ceasing,
Glory in thy perfect love.

Finish, then, thy new creation;
Pure and spotless let us be;
Let us see thy great salvation
Perfectly restored in thee;
Changed from glory into glory
Till in Heav'n we take our place,
Till we cast our crowns before thee,
Lost in wonder, love, and praise!

13

Epilogue

These things I [Jesus] have spoken to you so that in Me you may
have peace. In the world you have tribulation, but take courage; I
have overcome the world.

JOHN 16:33

YOGI BERRA WAS A pretty good baseball player and coach. He also
had a way with words, and his witticisms—some would say mala-
propisms—have been known to cause smiles to break out even on
the most dour of faces. For example, as mentioned in the preface,
he once said, "You got to be very careful if you don't know where
you're going because you might not get there." And on another
occasion he remarked, "We may be lost but we're making good
time." Both quips have more than a touch of humor in them. At
the same time, both of these sayings also express a heartbreaking
truth about the state of Western society. We are lost, and yet we
are speeding along at a frenetic pace in our terrible hurry to get
somewhere. However, since we don't seem to have the slightest
idea of where we should be going, we are not getting any closer to
any known desirable destination.

When I ask my students what they want in life, they all say
they want to be happy. So, I ask them what they need to be happy.

Usually, they tell me the most important need is the love of family and friends. They also tell me that they want peace—not just the cessation of hostilities, but deep inner peace. In fact, most people I talk to say the same thing—they want peace in their lives.

The Bible tells us that Jesus came to bring this peace. He came to reconcile God and man, and he did this by paying the price for our sin and selfishness. He laid down his life on the cross so that we could be reconciled with our heavenly Father—so that we could once again know his extravagant love.

Many people, however, have been scammed by the prince of scammers, and they don't give much attention to the One who can actually give them peace. Instead, they continue to be controlled by their fears. They spend their lives chasing after idols, especially Mammon. They nurture their grudges, refuse to forgive, and they try to take God's place on the throne of judgment. Or perhaps they acknowledge that God is on the throne, but instead of serving as his ambassadors and ministers of reconciliation, they enlist as soldiers in the culture wars. As a result, they have become spiritually deaf and blind, and they have no peace. We should not be surprised, therefore, when we read that the use of antidepressants and antianxiety medications has exploded in recent decades.[1]

Are you at peace? If not, why? Does fear and/or anger still control your thoughts and actions? What idols do you serve? Are you engaged in one form of battle or another with other members of the human race? What has all this striving gained for you? Are you lost but making good time? If so, is it worth the price that you are paying in stress, high blood pressure, sleepless nights? Why not let go of these things that actually hold on to and control you? Let go, and entrust your life to the God of peace, and let him make you one of his ambassadors and a minister of reconciliation.

Jesus is known as the Lamb of God. He was the unblemished Passover lamb that was sacrificed in our place for our sins. There is an interesting fact about sheep: they are naturally immune to the venom of pit vipers. In fact, their blood is used to make the

---

1. Wehrwein, "Astounding Increase."

antivenom that is used to treat many snake bites![2] This fallen world in which we live is ruled by the chief serpent, and his venom is deadly. Have you been healed by the blood of the Lamb of God? If not, what are you waiting for?

Philippians 4:6–7

Do not be anxious about anything, but in everything by prayer and pleading with thanksgiving let your requests be made known to God. And the peace of God, which surpasses all comprehension, will guard your hearts and minds in Christ Jesus.

2. Hart, "Blood of Sheep." See also ABC News, "Sheep's Blood."

Bibliography

ABC News. "Sheep's Blood Provides Rattlesnake Anti-Venom." May 22, 2005. https://www.abc.net.au/news/2005-05-23/sheeps-blood-provides-rattlesnake-anti-venom/1576314.

Augustine. *Confessions*. Translated by R. S. Pine-Coffin. Harmondsworth, UK: Penguin, 1975.

Barna, George. *America at the Crossroads: Explosive Trends Shaping America's Future and What You Can Do About It*. Grand Rapids: Baker, 2016.

———. *Barna Trends 2017: What's New and What's Next at the Intersection of Faith and Culture*. Grand Rapids: Baker, 2017.

Barra, Allen. *Yogi Berra: Eternal Yankee*. New York: Norton, 2009.

Byrne, Mary E., trans. "Be Thou My Vision." Versified by Eleanor H. Hull. Hymnary, 1927. https://hymnary.org/text/be_thou_my_vision_o_lord_of_my_heart.

Cyre, Susan A. *From Genesis to Revelation God Takes a Bride: The Divine Marriage of Which Human Marriage Is an Image*. New York: Page, 2019.

Dickerson, Matthew, and Susan Nop. "No Other Name." Track 1 on *Streams of Mercy*. Self-published, 2013. https://www.discogs.com/release/31135652-Matthew-Dickerson-2-Susan-Nop-Streams-of-Mercy?srsltid=AfmBOopvCxN2T_Fmu8ZUHS2GZpf3V96pl-1R49Z-baeLaKrm-SlrwmiS%3E.%20or%20%3Chttps://www.amazon.ca/Streams-Mercy-Matthew-Dickerson/dp/B099Q3H8LM.

Dickerson, Will. *The Fingerprint of God: Reflections on Love and Its Practice*. Eugene, OR: Resource, 2021.

Etymonline. "Devil (n.)." https://www.etymonline.com/word/devil.

Fawcett, John. "Blest Be the Tie That Binds." Hymnary, 1782. https://hymnary.org/text/blest_be_the_tie_that_binds.

Foster, Richard J. "The Danger of Spiritual Disciplines: Seven Pitfalls to Avoid." Renovaré, December 2024. https://renovare.org/articles/danger-of-spiritual-disciplines.

Haidt, Jonathan. *The Anxious Generation: How the Great Rewiring of Childhood Is Causing an Epidemic of Mental Illness*. New York: Penguin, 2024.

Harned, Lena Surzhko. "Holy Wars: How a Cathedral of Guns and Glory Symbolizes Putin's Russia." The Conversation, Mar. 2, 2022. https://theconversation.com/holy-wars-how-a-cathedral-of-guns-and-glory-symbolizes-putins-russia-176786.

Hart, Jeremy. "Blood of Sheep Protects Against Tongue of Viper." Independent, Feb. 7, 1994. https://www.the-independent.com/life-style/health-and-families/health-news/health-blood-of-sheep-protects-against-tongue-of-viper-there-may-be-no-rattlesnakes-in-wales-but-researchers-on-a-small-carmarthen-farm-may-save-some-of-the-two-million-people-worldwide-1392764.html.

Havergal, Frances Ridley. "Take My Life, and Let It Be." Hymnary, 1874. https://hymnary.org/text/take_my_life_and_let_it_be.

Herbert, George. "The Hold-fast." Poetry Foundation. https://www.poetryfoundation.org/poems/44363/the-hold-fast.

Johns Hopkins Medicine. "Forgiveness: Your Health Depends on It." https://www.hopkinsmedicine.org/health/wellness-and-prevention/forgiveness-your-health-depends-on-it.

Keller, W. Phillip. *A Shepherd Looks at Psalm 23*. Grand Rapids: Zondervan, 1970.

Kelly, Henry Ansgar. *Satan: A Biography*. Cambridge: Cambridge University Press, 2006.

Kunich, John C., and Richard I. Lester. "Profile of a Leader: The Wallenberg Effect." *Journal of Leadership Studies* 1 (1994) 94–107. https://doi.org/10.1177/107179199400100209.

Larson, Luke. "Faith, Politics, and Paradox in Culturally Christian Hungary." The Catholic World Report, June 9, 2023. https://www.catholicworldreport.com/2023/06/09/faith-politics-and-paradox-in-culturally-christian-hungary/.

Lewis, C. S. *The Lion, the Witch, and the Wardrobe*. New York: HarperCollins, 2025.

———. *The Screwtape Letters*. New York: HarperCollins, 2001.

Logos Staff. "The Apostles' Creed: Its History and Origins." Logos, Jan. 18, 2022. https://www.logos.com/grow/the-apostles-creed-its-history-and-origins/.

Luther, Martin. "A Mighty Fortress." Hymnary, 1529. https://hymnary.org/text/a_mighty_fortress_is_our_god_a_bulwark.

Mayo Clinic. "Forgiveness: Letting Go of Grudges and Bitterness." Nov. 22, 2022. https://www.mayoclinic.org/healthy-lifestyle/adult-health/in-depth/forgiveness/art-20047692.

Nelson, Jill. "Moscow Continues Targeting Christians in Russian-Occupied Territories." Christianity Today, Jan. 24, 2025. https://www.christianitytoday.com/2025/01/moscow-christians-russian-occupied-territories-persecution-orthodox/?fbclid=IwY2xjawIorelleHRuA2F lbQIxMQABHWL97gFgn2FT5HAfKh4hA7JQz3smFF2e32rwJDG-rhwXA6qsqouCCeqvt9A_aem_9lLVgfCKP_wt8Q3_1Kfgsw.

Bibliography

Nelson, Ryan. "Who Was Simon the Zealot? The Beginner's Guide." Overview Bible, Aug. 7, 2019. https://overviewbible.com/simon-the-zealot/.

Newton, John. "Amazing Grace! (How Sweet the Sound)." Hymnary, 1779. https://hymnary.org/hymn/AAHH2001/271.

O'Donnell, James J. *Pagans: The End of Traditional Religion and the Rise of Christianity*. New York: HarperCollins, 2015.

Sahgal, Neha, and Alan Cooperman. "Religious Belief and National Belonging in Central and Eastern Europe." Pew Research Center, May 10, 2017. https://www.pewresearch.org/religion/2017/05/10/religious-belief-and-national-belonging-in-central-and-eastern-europe/.

———. "2. Religious Commitment and Practices." Pew Research Center, May 10, 2017. https://www.pewresearch.org/religion/2017/05/10/religious-commitment-and-practices/.

Schoenian, Susan. "Feeding and Watering Equipment." Sheep 201, last updated Apr. 19, 2021. https://www.sheep101.info/201/feedwaterequip.html.

Spafford, Horatio Gates. "When Peace, Like a River" [It Is Well with My Soul]. Hymnary, 1873. https://hymnary.org/text/when_peace_like_a_river_attendeth_my_way.

Tolkien, J. R. R. *The Fellowship of the Ring*. Part 1 of The Lord of the Rings. New York: Bookspan, 2001.

Travers, Mark. "Expressing Gratitude Has Physical Health Benefits As Well As Emotional Benefits." Forbes, Nov. 27, 2020. https://www.forbes.com/sites/traversmark/2020/11/27/expressing-gratitude-has-physical-health-benefits-as-well-as-emotional-benefits/?sh=7d2986692559.

Wehrwein, Peter. "Astounding Increase in Antidepressant Use by Americans." Harvard Health Publishing, Oct. 20, 2011. https://www.health.harvard.edu/blog/astounding-increase-in-antidepressant-use-by-americans-201110203624.

Wesley, Charles. "Love Divine, All Loves Excelling." Hymnary, 1747. https://hymnary.org/text/love_divine_all_love_excelling_joy_of_he.

———. "O for a Thousand Tongues to Sing." Hymnary, 1739. https://hymnary.org/hymn/NNBH2001/23.

———. "Thou Hidden Source of Calm Repose." Hymnary, 1749. https://hymnary.org/text/thou_hidden_source_of_calm_repose.

Wikipedia. "Mammon." Last updated Feb. 26, 2025. https://en.wikipedia.org/wiki/Mammon#cite_note-Webster-2.

———. "Simon the Zealot." Last updated Mar. 18, 2025. https://en.wikipedia.org/wiki/Simon_the_Zealot.

Wiktionary. "κοιμητήριον." Last updated Mar. 30, 2025. https://en.wiktionary.org/wiki/%CE%BA%CE%BF%CE%B9%CE%BC%CE%B7%CF%84%CE%AE%CF%81%CE%B9%CE%BF%CE%BD.

Also available from Wipf and Stock

Will Dickerson

THE FINGERPRINT
OF GOD

Reflections on Love and Its Practice

https://wipfandstock.com/9781666704877/
the-fingerprint-of-god/

www.ingramcontent.com/pod-product-compliance
Lightning Source LLC
Chambersburg PA
CBHW060402090426
42734CB00011B/2234